T0245936

Connections

Worship
Companion

Year B, Volume 2

Season after Pentecost

# Connections

Worship
Companion

David Gambrell, editor

 WESTMINSTER
JOHN KNOX PRESS
LOUISVILLE • KENTUCKY

First Edition
Published by Westminster John Knox Press
Louisville, Kentucky

24 25 26 27 28 29 30 31 32 33—10 9 8 7 6 5 4 3 2 1

Book design by Drew Stevens
Cover design by Allison Taylor

Library of Congress Cataloging-in-Publication Data

Names: Gambrell, David, editor.
Title: Connections worship companion : Year C / David Gambrell.
Description: First edition. | Louisville, Kentucky : Westminster John Knox
   Press, 2021. | Series: Connections: a lectionary commentary for
   preaching and worship | Includes index. | Summary: "Part of the
   Connections commentary series, these worship resources help
   congregations illuminate the connections between Scripture and
   liturgical rhythms. A "Making Connections" essay precedes each
   liturgical season's resources, providing context for worship within the
   themes and purpose of the season"-- Provided by publisher.
Identifiers: LCCN 2021023009 (print) | LCCN 2021023010 (ebook) | ISBN
   9780664264963 (hardback) | ISBN 9781646982080 (ebook)
Subjects: LCSH: Common lectionary (1992). Year C. | Public worship. |
   Worship programs.
Classification: LCC BV199.L42 C66 2021 (print) | LCC BV199.L42 (ebook) |
   DDC 264.05--dc23
LC record available at https://lccn.loc.gov/2021023009
LC ebook record available at https://lccn.loc.gov/2021023010

Connections Worship Companion, Year B, Volume 2
ISBN: 9780664264956 (hardback)
ISBN: 9781646983780 (ebook)

Most Westminster John Knox Press books are available at special quantity
discounts when purchased in bulk by corporations, organizations, and special-interest
groups. For more information, please e-mail SpecialSales@wjkbooks.com.

Contents

Supplements for the Narrative Lectionary

Introduction

This is not a book of prayers—
at least not yet.

These words will not become prayers
until the Holy Spirit breathes them,
until the body of Christ speaks and hears them,
until the people of God live them
in acts of service and love.

These words come from different people
in different places of ministry—
pastors and poets,
students and scholars,
activists and artists,
evangelists and educators,
bakers and baristas,
mission workers and musicians.

They have different voices,
and those voices will resonate
with different worshipers
in different ways.

It will be up to you,
as a planner and leader of worship,
to make these words sing:

to pray them
among the beloved people of God
with honesty, passion, wonder, and grace;

to enact them
as the whole body of Christ
with heart, mind, soul, and strength;

to transform them
through the gifts of the Spirit,
with rhythm, color, texture, and taste.

You are encouraged, then,
even challenged,
even required
to find your own voice,
to inhabit these texts,
to adapt them as needed,
so that these words
may become the prayers
of your people
in your place
for the sake of the world,
all people,
in every place.

Only then
will these words become prayers.

Only then
will they rise like incense before God,
joining the intercession
of our great high priest,
Christ Jesus,
who still teaches us to pray.

David Gambrell

How to Use This Book

Three kinds of materials are provided in this volume. First, at the beginning of each major section is a short essay titled "Making Connections." These brief passages of commentary have several purposes:

- they introduce the primary theological themes of a given time in the Christian year;
- they highlight a particular biblical text, drawn from the lectionary, that may be used as a kind of lens for magnifying and examining the themes of the season;
- they point to distinctive features of the lectionary cycle included in this volume; and

- they offer practical and pastoral guidance for leaders as they seek to prepare faithful, thoughtful, creative, and engaging worship for the people of God.

These essays can be used in discussion with worship committees, planning teams, or church staff groups to promote biblical study, inspire theological reflection, and inform liturgical action.

Second, each section includes a collection of seasonal/repeating resources. These are liturgical texts intended for use during a certain span of time in the Christian year, whether occasionally or for several weeks in a row. Specifically, these resources include the following acts of worship:

> Confession and Pardon
> Prayer for Illumination
> Thanksgiving for Baptism
> Great Thanksgiving
> Prayer after Communion
> Prayer of Thanksgiving (for the dedication of the offering when the Eucharist is not celebrated)
> Blessing

These texts are somewhat broader and more general in their theological content and liturgical language, and they are designed for multiple uses within a liturgical season or period of Ordinary Time. They promote diachronic (meaning "through time") connections from one Sunday to the next, deriving their benefit from regular engagement with the church's tradition as people return to worship from week to week. They emphasize central convictions of Christian faith and life, supporting the kind of faith formation that takes place through sustained, long-term participation in worship. These texts are especially connected with the celebration of the sacraments.

Third, there is a set of resources for each Sunday or festival in the Christian year. Specifically, these resources include the following elements of the service:

> Opening Sentences (or Call to Worship)
> Prayer of the Day (or Gathering Prayer)
> Invitation to Discipleship
> Prayers of Intercession
> Invitation to Offering
> Invitation to the Table
> Charge

These texts are somewhat narrower and more specific in their theological content and liturgical language, and they are designed for use on a given Sunday or festival in the Christian year. They promote synchronic (meaning "same time") connections between the liturgy and the lectionary, deriving their benefit from flashes of insight that collect around a common word, image, or phrase from the biblical texts for the day. They emphasize particular practices of Christian faith and life, supporting the kind of faith formation that takes place in more concentrated, short-term experiences of worship. These texts are especially connected with the proclamation of the word.

By combining the **seasonal/repeating resources (in bold type)** with the *Sunday/festival elements (in italics)*, as well as other elements not provided in this resource (in regular type), as indicated below, worship planners will be able to assemble complete orders of worship for the Lord's Day.

GATHERING

> *Opening Sentences*
> Hymn, Psalm, or Spiritual Song
> *Prayer of the Day*
> **Confession and Pardon**

WORD

> **Prayer for Illumination**
> Scripture
> Sermon
> Hymn, Psalm, or Spiritual Song
> Affirmation of Faith
> *Invitation to Discipleship*
> **Thanksgiving for Baptism**
> *Prayers of Intercession*

EUCHARIST	[IF THE EUCHARIST IS OMITTED]
Invitation to Offering	*Invitation to Offering*
Offering	Offering
Invitation to the Table	
Great Thanksgiving	**Prayer of Thanksgiving**
Communion	
Prayer after Communion	

SENDING

> Hymn, Psalm, or Spiritual Song
> **Blessing** and *Charge*

This order of worship is offered as one example. The actions and elements of worship may of course be arranged in a variety of other ways according to denominational patterns and congregational practices. This resource is also available in ebook format, from which users can copy and paste liturgies for use in bulletins and other worship materials.

Lectionary Readings

This resource is designed to support and equip users of the three-year Revised Common Lectionary (1992), developed by the ecumenical Consultation on Common Texts as an adaptation and expansion of the Common Lectionary (1983). The contents and composition of this volume reflect that emphasis, consistent with the Connections commentary series.

However, this resource also includes supplemental liturgical materials for the four-year Narrative Lectionary (2010), designed by faculty at Luther Seminary in St. Paul, Minnesota. Taking advantage of overlap between the two systems, with these supplemental materials, this resource will address (at least obliquely) all of the primary texts of the Narrative Lectionary over the course of its six volumes.

See the Scripture index for the list of the lectionary readings supported in this volume (in canonical order). A comprehensive biblical index for both lectionaries will be published when all six volumes of the *Connections Worship Companion* have been completed.

Acknowledgments

Contributors to this volume include Claudia L. Aguilar Rubalcava, Mamie Broadhurst, Marci Auld Glass, Marcus A. Hong, Kimberly Bracken Long, Emily McGinley, Kendra L. Buckwalter Smith, Samuel Son, Slats Toole, and Byron A. Wade. Their deep faith, pastoral wisdom, creative gifts, and fervent prayers are the lifeblood of this work. The editor also expresses deep gratitude to David Maxwell, vice president for curriculum and church resources at Westminster John Knox Press, for his guidance in the development of this project, and to Jessica Miller Kelley, senior acquisitions editor at Westminster John Knox Press, for shepherding it to completion.

Key to Symbols and Abbreviations

Regular	Leader
Bold	People
Italics	Rubric describing liturgical action or identifying options
. . .	Time for individual prayers, spoken or silent
or	Alternate readings or responses

Resources for the Revised Common Lectionary

SEASON AFTER PENTECOST

Making Connections

In the time after Pentecost, Year B of the Revised Common Lectionary follows the life, teaching, and ministry of Jesus according to the Gospel of Mark, along with selections from the Gospel of John. Significant and distinctive passages from Mark include the symbol of new wineskins (Mark 2:13–22), disputes about the Sabbath (2:23–3:6), a house divided (3:20–35), the growing seed (4:26–34), the death of John the baptizer (6:14–29), controversies around purity (7:1–8, 14–15, 21–23), the Syrophoenician woman (7:24–37), welcoming children (9:30–37), teaching about marriage (10:2–16), the difficulty of salvation (10:17–31), the sons of Zebedee (10:35–45), the healing of Bartimaeus (10:46–52), and the widow's gift (12:38–44). Beginning with Proper 12, there is a five-week detour through the sixth chapter of the Gospel of John, where Jesus feeds five thousand and walks on the sea (John 6:1–21), then teaches about the bread of heaven (6:24–58) and the word of life (6:59–69). Worship planners might find creative ways to connect these readings with the church's proclamation of the Word and celebration of the sacraments. In the final weeks of the Christian year, the lectionary readings anticipate Advent by highlighting eschatological concerns: the birth pangs of the realm of God (Mark 13:1–8) and the nature of Jesus' kingdom (John 18:33–37). This presents an opportunity to preach and pray about the nature of Christian hope as we watch for Christ's coming again in glory.

There are two tracks of readings from the Old Testament in the time after Pentecost: the *semicontinuous* readings, which move in sequence through major stories and themes of the Hebrew Scriptures, and the *complementary* readings, which are connected with the events and images of Gospel readings. The semicontinuous readings in Year B cover a broad swath of biblical narrative and teaching. Roughly half of these readings (fifteen weeks) are devoted to the reigns of Saul, David, and Solomon in 1 Samuel, 2 Samuel, and 1 Kings. Another series of readings features the wisdom literature (eight weeks) of Song of Solomon, Proverbs, and Job, as well as the stories of women (three weeks) in the books of Esther and Ruth. Prominent themes include God's covenant with the house of David, the faith and faithfulness of biblical women, and the problem of evil. In this time after Pentecost, worship planners might find imaginative ways to recount the sagas of the rulers of Israel, to explore the experiences of women in Scripture, and to ponder the struggle and suffering of Job. The complementary readings in Year B, selected in coordination with the Gospel reading, come from a great array of Old Testament books: Genesis, Exodus, Numbers, Deuteronomy, Joshua, 1 Kings, 2 Kings, Job, Proverbs, Isaiah, Jeremiah, Lamentations, Ezekiel, Daniel, and Amos. These intertextual connections demonstrate how the whole canon of Scripture bears witness to Jesus as God's Word made flesh.

In the design of the Revised Common Lectionary, psalms and canticles (other biblical songs) are intended to be musical and prayerful responses to the first reading (typically Hebrew Scripture, or Acts during the season of Easter). Preachers will find strong connections between the first reading and the psalm or canticle; however, remember that the psalms and canticles are specific to their Old Testament track (semicontinuous or complementary) and thus not interchangeable. Worship planners might use the lectionary psalms and canticles in guiding the choice of hymns for the day, drawing on metrical settings of the psalms, for example.

The second readings present a series of sequential selections from New Testament epistles, featuring 2 Corinthians (seven weeks), Ephesians (seven weeks), James (five weeks), and Hebrews (seven weeks). Significant theological themes in Year B include weakness and strength, reconciliation, faith and works, and the priesthood of Christ. Worship planners might be attentive for ways to draw on these connections in the second half of the Christian year.

At the beginning of the time after Pentecost, on Trinity Sunday of Year B, we hear the promise of God's great love for the world—sending the only Son that the world might be saved through him (John 3:1–17). As Year B concludes on Christ the King/Reign of Christ Sunday, Jesus reveals to Pontius Pilate that the realm of God transcends this world (John 18:33–37). Jesus says, "My kingdom is not from this world. . . . For this I was born, and for this I came into the world, to testify to the truth. Everyone who belongs to the truth listens to my voice" (John 18:36a, 37). The great love of God extends to all people, embraces all creation, encompasses heaven and earth. This is "the good news of Jesus Christ" (Mark 1:1)—the Word we proclaim to the world.

Seasonal/Repeating Resources

These resources are intended for regular use throughout the time after Pentecost.

CONFESSION AND PARDON

1 Based on Isaiah 6:1–8; especially appropriate for Trinity Sunday

The confession and pardon may be led from the baptismal font.

> Do not be afraid; draw near to the Lord.
> Touch the hem of God's robe and be healed.
>
> Let us confess our sin.

The confession may begin with a time of silence for personal prayer.

> **Holy, holy, holy Lord of hosts,**
> **the earth is full of your glory.**
> **Have mercy on us, for we are lost—**
> **not fit to stand in your presence.**
> **We are people of unclean lips—**
> **failing to teach the truth,**
> **making promises in vain,**
> **spreading falsehood and fear.**
>
> **Forgive us, God of grace.**
> **Transform our lives with your mercy;**
> **open our lips to sing your praise.**
> **Send us out in your service,**
> **that we may proclaim your glory**
> **to all the people of the earth;**
> **through Jesus Christ we pray.**

Water may be poured or lifted from the baptismal font.

> The Lord reaches out with compassion.
> Our guilt has departed
> and our sin is blotted out.
>
> In the name of Jesus Christ we are forgiven.
> **Thanks be to God.**

2 Based on 2 Corinthians; especially appropriate for Propers 3–9

The confession and pardon may be led from the baptismal font.

> This is the day of our salvation.
> Now is the time for our deliverance!
>
> The grace of God has not come in vain.
> Let us confess our sin.

The confession may begin with a time of silence for personal prayer.

> **God of grace, we confess**
> **that we have failed to follow you.**
> **We rejoice in our own abundance**
> **and ignore the needs of our neighbors.**
> **We cite the letter of the law**
> **and forget the way of your Spirit.**
> **We boast about our strengths**
> **and try to hide our weaknesses.**
>
> **Forgive us, O Lord.**
> **Set us free from our sin**
> **and lead us to our salvation.**
> **Transform us by your grace,**
> **that we may live to share your love.**
> **Open our hearts to one another**
> **as you have opened your heart to us;**
> **through Jesus Christ our Savior.**

Water may be poured or lifted from the baptismal font.

If anyone is in Christ, there is a new creation:
everything old has passed away;
see, everything has become new!

In the name of Jesus Christ, we are forgiven.
Thanks be to God.

3 Based on Hebrews; especially appropriate for Propers 22–28

The confession and pardon may be led from the baptismal font.

Christ Jesus sympathizes with our weakness,
for he has been tested as we are, yet without sin.

Let us approach the throne of grace with boldness,
so that we may receive mercy from the Lord.

The confession may begin with a time of silence for personal prayer.

**You alone, O Lord, can judge
the thoughts and intentions of our hearts.
Nothing is hidden from your sight.
Before you everything is laid bare—
our captivity to sin and evil,
our devotion to false idols,
our neglect for neighbors in need,
our abuse of your creation,
our wandering from your way,
our failure to live by faith.**

**Forgive us, we pray.
Write your word upon our hearts.
Keep us faithful in your covenant.
Guide us in your new and living way.
All this we pray through Jesus Christ,
our great high priest in the house of God.**

Water may be poured or lifted from the baptismal font.

The Holy Spirit has spoken:
"I will remember their sins and lawless deeds no more."
Now our hearts are cleansed from all evil
just as our bodies are washed with water.
We can live in hope, confidence, and joy,
for God, who has promised, is faithful.

In the name of Jesus Christ, we are forgiven.
Thanks be to God.

PRAYER FOR ILLUMINATION

1 Based on John 6; especially appropriate for Propers 12–16

The prayer for illumination is led from the lectern or pulpit.

Lord Jesus Christ,
you have the words of eternal life.
Feed us with the gift of your grace
and fill us with the life of your Spirit,
that we may come to believe in you,
the Holy One of God. **Amen.**

2 Based on Proverbs and James; especially appropriate for Propers 17–21

The prayer for illumination is led from the lectern or pulpit.

Holy One,
your wisdom cries out in the street,
calling us to seek your will.
Teach us, by your Spirit,
to be doers of your word
and not merely hearers,
that our faith may bear good fruit
in works of service and love;
through Jesus Christ our Lord. **Amen.**

3 Based on Hebrews; especially appropriate for Propers 22–28

The prayer for illumination is led from the lectern or pulpit.

> God of our ancestors, for long generations
> you have spoken through the prophets;
> now you speak to us through your Son.
> By the work of your eternal Spirit,
> reveal to us your living and active word,
> that we may obey your will, hold fast to our faith,
> and enter into the sanctuary of your glory;
> through Christ Jesus, our great high priest. **Amen.**

THANKSGIVING FOR BAPTISM

1 Based on 2 Corinthians; especially appropriate for Propers 3–9

The thanksgiving for baptism is led from the baptismal font.

The introductory dialogue ("The Lord be with you . . .") may be sung or spoken.

> Lord of grace,
> God of love,
> Spirit of holy communion—
> we give you thanks and praise
> for our baptism in Christ Jesus.
>
> Through the gift of our baptism
> we no longer regard one another
> from a human point of view,
> but as beloved children of God
> and members of the body of Christ.
> Now we walk by faith, not by sight,
> confident in your saving love.
>
> Fill us with the life of your Spirit,
> that we may be afflicted but not crushed,
> perplexed but not driven to despair,
> persecuted but not forsaken,
> struck down but not destroyed—
> always carrying in our bodies
> the death and life of Jesus our Lord.

Let us share in the risen life of Christ.
Day by day renew us in your love,
that we may extend your grace to all.
Prepare us for your holy realm,
and lead us to our heavenly home:
the temple of the living God,
a house not made with human hands.

Lord of grace,
God of love,
Spirit of holy communion—
we give you thanks and praise
now and always. **Amen.**

2 Based on Ephesians; especially appropriate for Propers 10–16

The thanksgiving for baptism is led from the baptismal font.

The introductory dialogue ("The Lord be with you . . .") may be sung or spoken.

Blessed are you, O Lord our God,
for the gift of our baptism in Christ Jesus.
You have poured out your grace upon us
and claimed us as your beloved children.
You have made us one flesh, one body,
breaking down dividing walls of hostility.
You have made us citizens with the saints
and members of your holy household.

With the saints of every time and place
we pray for the work of your Spirit.
Fill us with the fullness of your love,
surpassing all human knowledge.
Equip us for the work of ministry,
for building up the body of Christ.
Make us tender, kind, and forgiving,
just as in Christ you have forgiven us.

Help us to live a life worthy of our calling
as we long for the fullness of time.
Clothe us with compassion and strength
to go and proclaim the gospel of peace.

Build your church into a holy temple,
a spiritual dwelling place for all.
Fill our hearts with songs of faith
and prayers of great thanksgiving.

Blessed are you, O Lord our God,
one God in the three persons,
Father, Son, and Holy Spirit,
above all, and through all, and in all. **Amen.**

3 Based on Mark 10:35–45; especially appropriate for Proper 24

The thanksgiving for baptism is led from the baptismal font.

The introductory dialogue ("The Lord be with you . . .") may be sung or spoken.

Lord Jesus Christ,
servant of the last and least,
we give you thanks and praise.
By your grace you serve us
with humility and compassion,
washing us clean from our sin.
Teach us to serve others.

Holy Spirit,
source and strength of all life,
we give you thanks and praise.
By your power you strengthen us
with the hope of your new creation,
pouring out your gifts among us.
Help us to strengthen others.

Eternal and Almighty One,
who welcomed the world into being,
we give you thanks and praise.
By your love you welcome us
as the people of your covenant,
claiming us as beloved children.
Lead us to welcome others.

For the gift and calling of our baptism
we give you thanks and praise—
Lord Jesus Christ,
Holy Spirit,
Eternal and Almighty One—
one God, now and forever. **Amen.**

GREAT THANKSGIVING

1 Based on John 6; especially appropriate for Propers 12–16

The Great Thanksgiving is led from the Communion table.

*In this eucharistic prayer, the responsive phrases ("Jesus is the bread of
life . . .") may be replaced with the Taizé song "Eat This Bread" or with
sung or spoken versions of the introductory dialogue ("The Lord be with
you . . ."), the Sanctus ("Holy, holy, holy . . ."), a memorial acclamation
("Christ has died . . ."), and a Trinitarian doxology and Great Amen.*

Jesus is the bread of life;
come to Christ and never hunger.

Jesus is the bread of life;
trust in Christ and never thirst.

In the wilderness we give you thanks, O God;
you fed us with manna from heaven,
sustaining your people on the journey
from slavery to freedom, death to life.
Now by your grace you give us
the bread that will never perish,
the food that endures for eternal life.

With all the saints of heaven and earth
we lift our voices in praise:
Jesus is the bread of life;
come to Christ and never hunger.

Jesus is the bread of life;
trust in Christ and never thirst.

Beside the sea we give you thanks, O God;
you fed a multitude with simple gifts,
satisfying the hunger of your people
with five barley loaves and two fish.
Now by your grace you give us
the bread that will never perish,
the food that endures for eternal life.

The words of institution are included here, if not elsewhere, while the bread and cup are lifted (but not broken/poured).

As we share this bread and cup,
receive our sacrifice of praise:
Jesus is the bread of life;
come to Christ and never hunger.

Jesus is the bread of life;
trust in Christ and never thirst.

In this place we give you thanks, O God;
you have poured out your life-giving Spirit,
transforming this bread, this cup, your people
into the body and blood of Christ.
Now by your grace you give us
the bread that will never perish,
the food that endures for eternal life.

Praise to you, holy triune God,
here and everywhere, now and always.
Jesus is the bread of life;
come to Christ and never hunger.

Jesus is the bread of life;
trust in Christ and never thirst.

2 Based on Ruth, 1 Samuel, Esther, Proverbs, Song of Solomon, Mark 5:21–43, Mark 7:24–37, and John 11:32–44; especially appropriate for Propers 8, 17–21, 26–28, and All Saints' Day

The Great Thanksgiving is led from the Communion table.

The introductory dialogue ("The Lord be with you . . .") may be sung or spoken.

> God of our mothers, we give you thanks
> for your steadfast love in all generations.
> Through the faithfulness of Naomi and Ruth
> you preserved us at the time of harvest.
> Through the persistence of Hannah
> you provided an answer to our prayers.
> Through the courage of Esther
> you protected us from evil and death.
>
> Therefore we worship you, singing our praise:

The Sanctus ("Holy, holy, holy . . .") may be sung or spoken.

> God of our sisters, we give you thanks
> for the goodness and grace of Jesus Christ.
> When a suffering woman in a crowd
> touched the fringe of your garment,
> you rewarded her faith with healing.
> When the daughter of a synagogue leader
> went down to the dust of death,
> you raised her up to new life.
> To the Syrophoenician woman
> you extended the table of your mercy,
> blessing all the peoples of the earth.
> To Mary and Martha of Bethany
> you revealed the good news of salvation:
> that Jesus is the resurrection and the life.

The words of institution are included here, if not elsewhere, while the bread and cup are lifted (but not broken/poured).

> Rejoicing in the voice of our beloved Savior,
> we lift up this bread and this cup
> as an offering of thanks and praise.

A memorial acclamation ("Christ has died . . .") may be sung or spoken.

> God of our daughters, pour out your Spirit
> upon the body of Christ in this place—
> in the bread, in the cup, and in your people.
> Nourish us with these gifts of grace,
> that we may grow in faith, hope, and love.
> Fill us with your Spirit of Wisdom,
> that we may cry out for righteousness and justice,
> provide for the family of faith,
> clothe the vulnerable with compassion,
> and open our hands to those in need.
> When the winter of life is past
> and the storms of sorrow are gone,
> call us home with songs of joy.
>
> All praise and thanks to you, Holy One—
> through the grace of Jesus Christ
> and in the unity of the Holy Spirit,
> one God, Mother of us all.

A Trinitarian doxology and Great Amen may be sung or spoken.

3 Based on Mark 12:28–34; especially appropriate for Proper 26

The Great Thanksgiving is led from the Communion table.

The introductory dialogue ("The Lord be with you . . .") may be sung or spoken.

> O Lord our God, we give you thanks.
> With heart and soul, with mind and strength,
> we praise your majesty, mercy, and might—
> your love for the world you created,
> your care for all creatures of the earth,
> your wisdom through the law and prophets,
> your power to set captives free.
>
> With all our neighbors on earth and in heaven,
> we sing to the glory of your holy name.

The Sanctus ("Holy, holy, holy . . .") may be sung or spoken.

O Lord our God, we thank you for Jesus.
With heart and soul, with mind and strength,
we remember his life and ministry—
his love for strangers and sinners,
his care for the poor and hungry,
his wisdom to teach your way,
his power to heal and save.

*The words of institution are included here, if not elsewhere, while the
bread and cup are lifted (but not broken/poured).*

This meal that we share in Jesus' name
is an offering of our love for you, O God.
Let it also be a witness to our neighbors
of your great love for all the world.

A memorial acclamation ("Christ has died . . .") may be sung or spoken.

O Lord our God, we pray for your Spirit.
With heart and soul, with mind and strength,
we call upon your transforming work:
in this bread and in this cup,
in the community of your people,
for the sake of the gospel
and for the life of the world.

Through the gift of your Spirit,
help us to serve you faithfully—
with love for all our neighbors,
with care for this wounded world,
with wisdom to speak the truth,
with power to strengthen the weak.

O Lord our God,
with heart and soul, with mind and strength,
we give you thanks,
we remember Jesus,
and we pray for your Spirit,
here and everywhere,
now and always. **Amen.**

A Trinitarian doxology and Great Amen may be sung or spoken.

PRAYER AFTER COMMUNION

1 Based on Mark 2–4; especially appropriate for Propers 3–6

The prayer after Communion is led from the Communion table.

> Christ Jesus, Lord of the sabbath,
> you have come to this house
> to eat and drink with us.
> You have fed us and filled us—
> with the grain of the field
> and the fruit of the vine,
> with the strength of your Word
> and the life of your Spirit.
> Now send us forth in service
> to share your gifts with others.
> Let us scatter the seed of justice
> and harvest the fruit of peace,
> all for the sake of your eternal realm
> and the glory of your holy name. **Amen.**

2 Based on Psalm 34; especially appropriate for Propers 14–16

The prayer after Communion is led from the Communion table.

> We bless you, O Lord.
> You have called us to this table
> to taste and see that you are good
> and to sing your thanks and praise.
> You have drawn near to us
> to satisfy our hunger and thirst
> and to save us from every trouble.
> Now send us forth from this feast
> to resist the power of evil
> and pursue the promise of peace.
> Fill us with your Holy Spirit
> to share your gifts of grace
> and proclaim your great love.
> All this we pray in Jesus' name. **Amen.**

3   Based on Isaiah 25:6–9; especially appropriate for All Saints' Day

The prayer after Communion is led from the Communion table.

> We give you thanks and praise, O God,
> for you have prepared a feast for us—
> the rich food of heavenly grace,
> the well-aged wine of salvation.
> You have wiped away our tears
> and taken away our disgrace.
> You have destroyed the shroud of sin
> and swallowed up death forever.
> Now send us out with gladness,
> rejoicing in the gift of salvation;
> through Jesus Christ our Lord. **Amen.**

PRAYER OF THANKSGIVING

1   Based on 2 Corinthians; especially appropriate for Propers 4–9

The prayer of thanksgiving may be led from the Communion table.

> Thank you, God of grace,
> for giving us this treasure in clay jars—
> light and life in Jesus Christ.
> Jesus became poor for our sake,
> that we might be rich in mercy.
> Let the power of Christ dwell in us
> as we share these gifts with others.
> Help us to proclaim the good news
> that your abundance is for everyone
> and your grace is sufficient for all;
> through Jesus Christ our Lord. **Amen.**

2 Based on John 6; especially appropriate for Propers 12–16

The prayer of thanksgiving may be led from the Communion table.

> We give you thanks and praise, O God.
> By the grace of the Lord Jesus Christ
> you take and bless our ordinary gifts
> and make of them an abundant feast.
> Teach us to share all that we have.
> Use our resources to feed multitudes.
> Help us to gather up the fragments
> so that nothing and no one may be lost;
> through Jesus Christ, the bread of life. **Amen.**

3 Based on Job; especially appropriate for Propers 22–25

The prayer of thanksgiving may be led from the Communion table.

> Glory, thanks, and praise to you, O God.
> You laid the foundation of the earth
> and determined its measurements.
> You set the cornerstone of the world
> when the morning stars sang together
> and the heavenly hosts shouted for joy.
> Receive the simple works of our hands
> and the humble offerings of our lives.
> Use them, in your goodness and mercy,
> that your purpose may be fulfilled
> for us, our neighbors, and all creation;
> through Jesus Christ our Lord. **Amen.**

BLESSING

1 Based on Romans 8:12–17; especially appropriate for Trinity Sunday

The blessing and charge may be led from the doors of the church.

> Children of promise and peace,
> may the grace of Abba God,
> the love of Jesus Christ,
> and the life of the Holy Spirit
> be with you now and always. **Alleluia!**

2 Based on Proverbs; especially appropriate for Propers 18–20

The blessing and charge may be led from the doors of the church.

> May the Wonder of God
> bless you with all beauty.
> May the Word of God
> guide you in all goodness.
> May the Wisdom of God
> teach you in all truth. **Alleluia!**

3 Based on Revelation 1:4b–8; especially appropriate for Christ the King/Reign of Christ Sunday

The blessing and charge may be led from the doors of the church.

> May the grace and peace of the Almighty—
> God who is
> and who was
> and who is to come—
> be with you all. **Alleluia!**

Trinity Sunday

Isaiah 6:1–8   Romans 8:12–17
Psalm 29   John 3:1–17

OPENING SENTENCES

> God of the many,
> speak that we might hear in one another
> the majesty of your creation.
> **Let us lift our many voices as one**
> **in praise and gratitude,**
> **trusting that in our collective voice**
> **we find collective liberation.**

PRAYER OF THE DAY

> God of the multitude,
> God of the Trinity,
> the Three-in-One:
> Tune our hearts to the harmony of your voice.
> Grant us the power to hear
> the distinctions of your notes
> without failing to attend
> to the chorus of who you are,
> that in our listening
> we might find our imaginations broadened
> for the sake of your transformative work within us. **Amen.**

> *Then I heard the voice of the Lord saying, "Whom shall I send, and who will go for us?" And I said, "Here am I; send me!"*
>
> *Isaiah 6:8*

INVITATION TO DISCIPLESHIP

The invitation to discipleship may be led from the baptismal font.

The power of God's voice reverberates
throughout all of creation,
and you are invited to join in!

How will you sing a song of salvation?
How will you be a voice of grace
in a world that struggles to sing along?
Receive this invitation to join in God's chorus,
and let yours be the voice
that helps us all sing with a fresh intonation.

PRAYERS OF INTERCESSION

The prayers of intercession may be led from the midst of the congregation.

God of the multitude,
who sees all of who we are
and all of who we have yet to be,
we lift up to you our limited scope
for imagining who you are
and what you desire for us.
We invite you to move in those spaces
and ways that confound our capacity
to find our way through.
By the powers of your being
let our world be drawn
to your vision of greater wholeness.

May the call of Christ,
which models for us what it means
to embody your radical hospitality,
urge us toward a more honest reckoning
of the ways in which we remain closed off
to one another, to ourselves, and to you.
May his enduring commitment to your vision
propel us toward a more courageous
and compassionate expression of faith.

Let your Spirit breathe fresh life and understanding
as we seek to renew our relationships
with one another.
Let her imagination be made evident
in our conceptions of who you are
and how we could be fruitful witnesses
of your transformative work within us and among us.

In your holy name we pray. **Amen.**

INVITATION TO OFFERING

The invitation to offering may be led from the Communion table.

Jesus offers us new ways of living
and doing life and faith.
In this moment, you are invited to consider
the abundance of this invitation
and to respond from a place
of your own abundance
through your own gifts.

Offer what you will,
not as an act of obligation
but as a reflection of gratitude
for what God promises to do
within us, among us, and through us.

INVITATION TO THE TABLE

The invitation to the table is led from the Communion table.

The apostle Paul teaches us
that the Spirit we have received through Christ
does not make us slaves to fear and anxiety;
rather, she advances our adoption
into the broader story
that God is writing across generations.

At this table we remember our adoption
into the family of God—
that we do not journey alone
but alongside one another
as disciples across space and time,
who encourage one another in the breaking of bread,
just as Jesus encouraged his followers so long ago.

CHARGE

The blessing and charge may be led from the doors of the church.

May the God who promises us new life
lead us from this place
with the courage to sing a new song,
that in our singing we might discover
the power of our own voice
and join it with others
for the sake of a world
that longs for fresh expressions
of life together and life abundant.
Amen. *or* **Thanks be to God.**

Proper 3

Sunday, May 24–28, if after Trinity Sunday

Hosea 2:14–20   2 Corinthians 3:1–6
Psalm 103:1–13, 22   Mark 2:13–22

OPENING SENTENCES

> O my whole being,
> all that is within me:
> **Bless God's holy name.**

> Come, bless the Holy One with me,
> for as high as the heavens are above the earth,
> **so great is God's steadfast love**
> **toward those who fear God.**

PRAYER OF THE DAY

> Merciful God,
> your steadfast love and faithfulness
> will not let you turn from us.
> You speak tenderly to us
> and to all your creation,
> longing for us to offer back to you
> a love letter, written on our hearts.
> O God, make us ministers of a new covenant,
> written not with ink
> but with your living, lively Spirit,
> who calls us to follow you
> with our whole selves
> in compassionate care for all your children
> and all creation.
> Help us to recognize those who are sick among us,
> and the sickness within ourselves.
> And enable us to craft, with you,
> a new healing—holy and whole,
> through the power of that same Spirit. **Amen.**

INVITATION TO DISCIPLESHIP

The invitation to discipleship may be led from the baptismal font.

God calls to us tenderly,
inviting us to follow
into a new covenant of generous love.

Will we become ministers of this new covenant,
writing our love not only with words
but with all that we do and all that we are?

PRAYERS OF INTERCESSION

The prayers of intercession may be led from the midst of the congregation.

O God, you have made your ways known to us
across time and space;
stories abound of your loving care.
Help us not to forget your compassion
for all of your children;
rather, in this moment,
encourage us to approach you with confidence,
trusting you with all that weighs heavy on our hearts.

God, we entrust to you
those stricken by all kinds of disease,
who ache in body and spirit,
and sorrow in beds and in silence.
**Grant to them, O blessed one,
caring hands and compassionate hearts,
vessels of your healing.**

God, we entrust to you
those in the pit of despair,
who witness the destruction of your creation
and the debasing of your children.
**Grant to them, O blessed one,
willing kindred spirits that seek repair,
and perseverance for the journey.**

God, we entrust to you
those longing for good things,
those who hunger for food and for justice
and who yearn for water and for peace.
Grant to them, O blessed one,
rest amid their restlessness,
and companions in their questing.

God, we entrust to you
those cast out and despised,
those who desire belonging and stability
and who seek a new home or a recognition of new identity.
Grant to them, O blessed one,
a community that knows them,
welcomes them, loves them.

O God, let our souls not forget all you have provided:
you forgive all iniquity,
you heal our diseases,
you redeem life from the Pit,
you crown us with steadfast love and mercy,
and you satisfy us with good as long as we live,
so that our youth is renewed like the eagle's.
O God, may we participate
in your answer to our prayers,
even as we wait with eagerness,
for your redemption of this whole world;
through Jesus Christ we pray. **Amen.**

INVITATION TO OFFERING

The invitation to offering may be led from the Communion table.

We have confidence through Christ toward God—
not that we bring anything of ourselves,
but that God has made us qualified
and has equipped us to participate in Christ's ministry.

Secure in that knowledge,
let us give from what God has provided.

INVITATION TO THE TABLE

The invitation to the table is led from the Communion table.

This is God's table,
where all are invited—
sinner and saint,
confident and questioning,
and many who are all of the above and more.
Here there is a clean cup,
fresh bread,
and a new covenant
for all of us to share.

All has been made ready;
come, let us partake of the feast.

CHARGE

The blessing and charge may be led from the doors of the church.

With all that you are,
show that you are a love letter of Christ,
written not with ink
but with the Spirit of the living God.
Amen. *or* **Thanks be to God.**

Proper 4

Sunday, May 29—June 4, if after Trinity Sunday

SEMICONTINUOUS READINGS

1 Samuel 3:1–10 (11–20)   2 Corinthians 4:5–12
Psalm 139:1–6, 13–18   Mark 2:23–3:6

OPENING SENTENCES

God has called us here,
each by our own name.
We hear your voice, O God.
We lift our voices to you.

Are you ready for God's re-creation?
We are your people, O God,
ready to play
and ready to work!

PRAYER OF THE DAY

God, whose eyesight never grows dim,
watch over us
and protect us from corruption.
Jesus, whose love never rests,
release us from our sin
and help us to accept your grace.
Spirit, whose light is deeper than vision
and whose fire never goes out,
help us to see Jesus' face
in our own faces
and in the faces of our neighbors. **Amen.**

---

*Now the boy Samuel was ministering to the LORD
under Eli. The word of the LORD was rare in those
days; visions were not widespread.*

1 Samuel 3:1

INVITATION TO DISCIPLESHIP

The invitation to discipleship may be led from the baptismal font.

God has entrusted the treasure of the gospel
to our dull clay hearts,
so that no one may doubt
the origin of the gospel's power.

Do you struggle with despair?
You are not disqualified.
Power to heal does not come from perfection.
Do you feel afflicted, crushed, perplexed?
Your brokenness and cracks
are windows letting out God's powerful light.

PRAYERS OF INTERCESSION

The prayers of intercession may be led from the midst of the congregation.

Is anything hidden before you, O God?
You know our sins and fears.
You also know our hopes and dreams.
Though the world might see little in us,
you see us as faithful servants
and call us to stand up for the world.
Guide our words and thoughts as we pray.

For humility,
that we might come clean
about our brokenness;
that we might not hide from you,
but face your truth and grace.

For confidence,
that we might know beyond a doubt
that we are fearfully and wonderfully made
by a good Creator,
whose image is indelibly marked in everyone;
that we might recognize your glory in ourselves,
just as we see it in others.

For the church,
that we might be confident
in the treasure you have given to us;
that we might remember
that the gospel does not lose value
because of what we lack.

For the world,
that every person might share
an innate love for your truth;
that we might not be tempted by false prophets,
but make the sacrifices necessary
to embrace your truth
and welcome your healing. **Amen.**

INVITATION TO OFFERING

The invitation to offering may be led from the Communion table.

Let us not put limits
on God's love for us and for the world.
Let us not put limits
on our love for God and for the world.
Let us not put limits
on how we give to God's work.

Every day is a day to do God's work.
Every resource we have is a resource for peace.
Let us make everything available
for God's good work.

INVITATION TO THE TABLE

The invitation to the table is led from the Communion table.

This is the table of the Lord.
The Lord has invited everyone.
But you must come as you are.
Be ready to come face to face
with your true self—
no disguises,
no self-deception at the table of God,
no self-condemnation before Jesus.

At this table we share the truth—
truth about our sins,
truth about our restoration.

CHARGE

The blessing and charge may be led from the doors of the church.

You are sent out with the great news
of God's redeeming love for the world.
This truth will cut hearts.
Some will resist. Some will repent.
Your calling is to preach it nevertheless—
with words and by your discipleship,
day by day.
Amen. *or* **Thanks be to God.**

Proper 4

Sunday, May 29—June 4, if after Trinity Sunday

COMPLEMENTARY READINGS

Deuteronomy 5:12–15   2 Corinthians 4:5–12
Psalm 81:1–10   Mark 2:23–3:6

OPENING SENTENCES

Sing aloud to God.
Sing praise to God!

For the Lord has freed us from every burden
and supplies our every need.
Sing praise!

PRAYER OF THE DAY

Gracious God,
who made the world and all that is in it,
we thank you for the gift of Sabbath
and your faithfulness to us all.
We are equally beloved in your eyes;
let us so love one another.
In Jesus' name we pray. **Amen.**

INVITATION TO DISCIPLESHIP

The invitation to discipleship may be led from the baptismal font.

If you have seen the light of Christ
and want to know him more, come.
If you seek to be healed, come.
If you long for a world that is just, come.

Jesus, the lover of us all,
welcomes you.

PRAYERS OF INTERCESSION

The prayers of intercession may be led from the midst of the congregation.

God of the Sabbath,
thank you for the gifts of rest
and freedom from our labors,
for making us all equal in your eyes,
for giving us a law of love.
In faithfulness to you,
we ask for your loving care for our world.

For the health of our planet:
[Name your local land and water.]
Creator of all, **hear our prayer.**

For the mission of your church,
in this congregation and around the world:
[Name the church's endeavors.]
Creator of all, **hear our prayer.**

For those who govern,
that they may lead with wisdom:
[Name local, national, and international leaders.]
Creator of all, **hear our prayer.**

For those who work to make the world more just:
[Name leaders, movements, and organizations.]
Creator of all, **hear our prayer.**

For peace in our countries,
our streets, and our homes:
[Name places of violence.]
Creator of all, **hear our prayer.**

For all in need of healing
of body, mind, or spirit:
[Name those who suffer.]
Creator of all, **hear our prayer.**

For the deep concerns of our hearts:
[Offer time for silent prayer.]
Creator of all, **hear our prayer.**

Thank you, O God, for hearing our prayers.
We entrust to you not only our concerns
but our very lives,
asking that you make us ever more faithful to you.
In the name of your Son and our Savior,
Jesus Christ. **Amen.**

INVITATION TO OFFERING

The invitation to offering may be led from the Communion table.

We have this treasure in clay jars—
the extraordinary power of God in Jesus Christ.

With grateful and joyful hearts
let us bring our gifts to God.

INVITATION TO THE TABLE

The invitation to the table is led from the Communion table.

Christ invites all who hunger
to come to his table.
Here is the bread of life;
here is the cup of salvation.
Just as our God fed us
in the desert and on hillsides,
in upper rooms and lakeshores,
so does God feed us here.

Come; there is a place for you here.

CHARGE

The blessing and charge may be led from the doors of the church.

Forgiven, freed, and fed,
go to share the light and love of Christ.
Amen. *or* **Thanks be to God.**

Proper 5

Sunday, June 5–11, if after Trinity Sunday

SEMICONTINUOUS READINGS

1 Samuel 8:4–11 (12–15),   2 Corinthians 4:13–5:1
  16–20 (11:14–15)   Mark 3:20–35
Psalm 138

OPENING SENTENCES

I give thanks to God,
who unseats rulers.
God rescues the oppressed.

I praise God,
who removes dictators.
God's power topples false powers.

PRAYER OF THE DAY

God, our one true Lord,
you seek our devotion
so we won't give it to others
who would abuse us.
Help us to submit to your meekness.
Jesus, our one true Savior,
you have shared with us
your resurrection power,
making new life a reality
in the darkest despair.
Help us to welcome you with wonder.
Spirit, our one true Sustainer,
grant us the power to resist
the forces that kill,
and grant us love's capacity
to let go of our own false strength.
Help us to rest in your peace. **Amen.**

INVITATION TO DISCIPLESHIP

The invitation to discipleship may be led from the baptismal font.

What does it mean to call Jesus our sibling?
It is to follow him in word and deed,
to feed the hungry, to heal the sick,
to take in those rejected by the world,
to love and cherish those deemed useless.
To be Jesus' family
is to resist all the demonic powers
that keep people down—
through crushing racism, sexism,
and other dividing "isms."

This is the family of Jesus.
You are invited to join us in this family.

PRAYERS OF INTERCESSION

The prayers of intercession may be led from the midst of the congregation.

God, we come to you
knowing that you can meet all of our desires.
We ask that you give
only what is good for us
and not what we desire.
We ask that you redeem our desires
even as we offer our fervent prayers.

We pray for the earth,
this beautiful interconnected life-web.
Help us to see our interdependence.
Help us to practice making space for each other
so that all things can thrive.

We pray for our church,
that we might be the church for all people.
Help us to be a community
where the afflicted
can be comforted,
where the despairing
can become hope for others,
where our crosses
become sources of salvation.

We pray for our neighbors;
though living next to each other,
we live as strangers,
afraid of the struggles
in our homes and hearts.
Help us to care,
and to receive care,
and to not fall into apathy.

We pray for our government.
Protect us from polarization and demonization.
Keep us from hateful and dishonest words.
Help us to be truthful and loving,
faithful in our conviction
while entrusting judgment to you.

All this we pray through Christ Jesus. **Amen.**

INVITATION TO OFFERING

The invitation to offering may be led from the Communion table.

Is there anything we earn by our own strength alone?
Even the ability to give is a gift from God.

As we share our gifts, let us remember
that giving is the truest recognition
of God's grace in our life—
for the more we give,
the more we understand grace.

INVITATION TO THE TABLE

The invitation to the table is led from the Communion table.

Jesus is the bread, the wine, the host.
Yet we have misunderstood and betrayed him.
We have called him everything but what he truly is—
the Savior, the Child of God.
Nevertheless, he calls us family
and makes a seat for us at the table.

We are family!
So come enjoy this meal,
and accept your place in the family of God.

CHARGE

The blessing and charge may be led from the doors of the church.

There is so much to tell the world.
We couldn't keep the good news to ourselves
even if we tried.
We have the word of life.
The gospel's power of life
is beaming and crackling with the power of God
and shining brightly through our cracks.
Amen. *or* **Thanks be to God.**

Proper 5

Sunday, June 5–11, if after Trinity Sunday

COMPLEMENTARY READINGS

Genesis 3:8–15   2 Corinthians 4:13–5:1
Psalm 130   Mark 3:20–35

OPENING SENTENCES

Wait for the Lord.
God is full of love
and promises to forgive.

Wait for the Lord.
Do not lose hope,
for God has come to save.

PRAYER OF THE DAY

God of grace, you create us in love
and supply all our needs.
You claim us as your own
in the waters of baptism.
You feed us at your own table
and bind us into one body.
All honor and praise to you, O God,
now and forever. **Amen.**

INVITATION TO DISCIPLESHIP

The invitation to discipleship may be led from the baptismal font.

Whoever does the will of God
is welcomed into the family of Jesus Christ.
Even when you turn from God,
God still waits for you.

If you long to be more faithful,
to be part of the family of Jesus
or to return to the fold, come.
Christ awaits with open arms.

PRAYERS OF INTERCESSION

The prayers of intercession may be led from the midst of the congregation.

Mighty God,
you created the world and called it good;
you made us to love you and one another.
Yet our world is broken and
in need of your care.
Healing God, **hear our prayer.**

For your church, here and around the world . . .
Reconcile our divisions
and strengthen our witness.
Healing God, **hear our prayer.**

For countries at war
and nations who threaten the peace . . .
Restore your justice
and bind up our wounds.
Healing God, **hear our prayer.**

For our nation . . .
Bridge our divides,
that we may work together for the common good.
Healing God, **hear our prayer.**

For our communities . . .
Foster understanding between those
who differ from one another,
that we might live in harmony.
Healing God, **hear our prayer.**

For those we love . . .
Soothe our hurts, heal our relationships,
and enable us to love one another well.
Healing God, **hear our prayer.**

For our secret concerns
and those troubles known only to you . . .
Healing God, **hear our prayer.**

We offer these prayers to you, O God,
and offer ourselves as your servants,
that we might be part of your healing work,
even as we wait for your eternal realm
of justice, peace, and love.
In the name of Jesus, our Savior and Friend,
we pray. **Amen.**

INVITATION TO OFFERING

The invitation to offering may be led from the Communion table.

In our baptism Jesus made us siblings
with him and one another.

With gratitude for that gift
and in obedience to his will,
let us bring our tithes and offerings to God.

INVITATION TO THE TABLE

The invitation to the table is led from the Communion table.

Even in the face of the trials and tribulations
of this life
we do not lose heart,
for Jesus Christ has made us his own
and invites us to gather at his table.
Whoever eats of this bread
will never be hungry;
whoever drinks of this cup
will never thirst.

Come, for Jesus waits to welcome you.

CHARGE

The blessing and charge may be led from the doors of the church.

Go in peace,
forgiving one another
as you have been forgiven.
Amen. *or* **Thanks be to God.**

Proper 6

Sunday, June 12–18, if after Trinity Sunday

SEMICONTINUOUS READINGS

1 Samuel 15:34–16:13   2 Corinthians 5:6–10 (11–13), 14–17
Psalm 20   Mark 4:26–34

OPENING SENTENCES

Praise God in your time of need.
God helps us.
We will not fall for false saviors.

Praise God, even in times of uncertainty.
God protects us.
We will walk by faith and not by sight.

PRAYER OF THE DAY

God the Farmer, seed your word
in the ground of our hearts.
Plant good seed that will bear
the fruits of abundant life.
Jesus the Farmer,
till our hearts and make them soft.
Make them vulnerable
so they can accept the seed,
the sun, and the rain.
Holy Spirit the Farmer,
pull out the weeds that choke
the new life you have planted.
May our lives bear the fruit of the gospel. **Amen.**

---

*[Jesus] also said, "The kingdom of God is as if
someone would scatter seed on the ground, and
would sleep and rise night and day, and the seed
would sprout and grow, he does not know how."*
Mark 4:26–27

INVITATION TO DISCIPLESHIP

The invitation to discipleship may be led from the baptismal font.

How mysterious is this life of discipleship!
The transformation of lives
is the work of God.
In the most unexpected places
you will meet saints,
people radiating God's love.

So don't discriminate in your discipleship.
Trust God, and be good to all people.
You will be surprised
at how the kingdom seed bears fruit in your life.

PRAYERS OF INTERCESSION

The prayers of intercession may be led from the midst of the congregation.

Jesus, you have given us
the joy of intercession—
that whatever we ask in your name,
you would do.
Taking up this awesome burden, we pray.

For your church in all nations . . .
that the church would boldly speak
and live out your truth,
confronting false powers at all costs,
even at the risk of censure and closure,
never ceasing to proclaim your message to the world.

For the leaders of nations . . .
that they would know their proper place
as humans and servants of God,
and that they would be about God's agenda
of making sure that all may flourish.

For migrants and refugees
who do not have a country to call their own
or a home to rest in . . .
that you would advocate for them,
that nations would welcome them,
and that people would make space for their stories.

For this earth and all its inhabitants . . .
that they would be fruitful and nourished,
that the air and the waters would be renewed,
that all living things
might breathe clean air and drink clean water
and join the chorus of creation
praising God, our Creator. **Amen.**

INVITATION TO OFFERING

The invitation to offering may be led from the Communion table.

The abundance of our life
is due to the seed and the work of the farmer.
Abundance is how God
gives us the gift of sharing.

Let us share our gifts, releasing our abundance
so that it may produce greater abundance.

INVITATION TO THE TABLE

The invitation to the table is led from the Communion table.

We come to the Lord's table,
for all of us must appear before
the judgment seat of Christ.
The judgment is both severe and gracious.
The meal is both conviction and pardon.
At this table you cannot pretend
to be someone you are not.
Unburdened with the need for deception,
come as yourself,
for you are the one Christ has called by name.

CHARGE

The blessing and charge may be led from the doors of the church.

We are given the seeds of life.
We have the plow to till the soil.
We have the energy that comes from abundance.
Wherever we go and whomever we meet,
let us share the abundance of the gospel,
the good news of God's unfailing love.
Amen. *or* **Thanks be to God.**

Proper 6

Sunday, June 12–18, if after Trinity Sunday

COMPLEMENTARY READINGS

Ezekiel 17:22–24   2 Corinthians 5:6–10 (11–13), 14–17
Psalm 92:1–4, 12–15   Mark 4:26–34

OPENING SENTENCES

> Give thanks to the Lord!
> **Sing praise to God's name!**
>
> For God is steadfast and faithful;
> the Lord is always righteous.
> **God is our rock;**
> **sing praise to the Lord!**

PRAYER OF THE DAY

> God of creation,
> you make all things flourish
> and give life to all.
> You create a place for those who seek you
> and give comfort to those in distress.
> Thank you for the ways you bless us
> and for the promise of your reign to come,
> where all shall be well
> and everyone shall find a home.
> In Jesus' name we pray. **Amen.**

INVITATION TO DISCIPLESHIP

> *The invitation to discipleship may be led from the baptismal font.*
>
> Jesus died that we might live;
> he was raised that we might be raised with him.
> Even now he is making all things new!
>
> If you seek new life,
> come to Christ
> and he will set you free.

The prayers of intercession may be led from the midst of the congregation.

God of life,
you create us in love,
you create us for love,
and you hear us when we pray to you.
We come with the troubles of the world
weighing heavy on our hearts
and seek your loving mercy.
God of life, **hear our prayer.**

For countries at war,
and all those who suffer;
for an end to violence
in deserts and mountains,
on city streets and in our homes,
God of life, **hear our prayer.**

For clean water to drink
and enough to share;
for clean air to breathe
and renewable energy;
for justice for all creatures of the earth,
God of life, **hear our prayer.**

For an end to bigotry
and acts of hate;
for those whose bodies
make them targets for persecution;
for all those who suffer
at the hands of bullies and abusers,
God of life, **hear our prayer.**

For your church,
divided and dismayed;
encourage us in faith
and strengthen our mission,
that we might follow you as true disciples.
God of life, **hear our prayer.**

For all those who are sick or dying,
for all who care for them;
grant them healing,
give them peace,
and uphold them in your love.
God of life, **hear our prayer.**

For our families and our friends,
all those who are close to our hearts;
bless them, embrace them,
and supply all their needs.
God of life, **hear our prayer.**

You are infinite in power and beauty, O God;
you are our rock, our hope, and our salvation.
Thank you for receiving our prayers,
and empower us to do your work
in this world you so love,
for Jesus' sake. **Amen.**

INVITATION TO OFFERING

The invitation to offering may be led from the Communion table.

It is good to give thanks to the Lord,
says the psalmist,
to declare God's love in the morning
and God's faithfulness at night.

With joy and gratitude,
let us bring our offerings to
our loving and faithful God.

INVITATION TO THE TABLE

The invitation to the table is led from the Communion table.

At this table
Jesus opens his arms wide,
inviting all who hunger and thirst,
accepting all who call on him,
loving all who seek him.

So come,
for Christ has prepared this feast for you.

CHARGE

The blessing and charge may be led from the doors of the church.

Go in peace,
giving thanks to God in every circumstance
and sharing the love of Christ wherever you go,
even as you watch and wait
for the realm that is to come.
Amen. *or* **Thanks be to God.**

Proper 7

Sunday, June 19–25, if after Trinity Sunday

SEMICONTINUOUS READINGS

1 Samuel 17:(1a, 4–11, 19–23) 32–49   2 Corinthians 6:1–13
  or 1 Samuel 17:57–18:5, 10–16   Mark 4:35–41
Psalm 9:9–20 *or* Psalm 133

OPENING SENTENCES

God never abandons the people.
The oppressed are not alone.
Sing praises to the Lord, who is just.

God comes and strengthens the weak.
God stands up with the poor.
Sing praises to the Lord, whom we can trust.

PRAYER OF THE DAY

Judge, fair and just,
you don't forget the cries of the weak.
You know what we need
and what we need to repent of.
Liberator, who was born poor
from a city without honor,
you shook the foundations
of the government and religion
that disregarded the needy.
Holy Advocate,
you are still bringing people together
and toppling giants that bully the weak.
We worship you,
rising up with great hope. **Amen.**

INVITATION TO DISCIPLESHIP

The invitation to discipleship may be led from the baptismal font.

Following Jesus,
we will face giant storms,
threats, and massive waves.
Don't be afraid.
Jesus is with us.
Jesus is Lord,
even above the giants we face.
Those massive threats dissipate
before his command.

There is no greater adventure
than the journey of discipleship—
living in God's just kingdom.

PRAYERS OF INTERCESSION

The prayers of intercession may be led from the midst of the congregation.

We are people of the God
whose love is at the center of all creation.
In rhythm with the heartbeat of God, we pray.

We lift up the church,
that the great people of God
in every corner of the world,
in local congregations and in the streets,
may not cower from threats of any kind;
that we may stand up for the powerless
and for God's glory.

We lift up the nations,
that they would not challenge God's rule
but would submit the laws of their lands
to the rule of God's love
and to the inviolable value of all living things.

We lift up those in oppression,
that they may witness their Redeemer;
those in sin,
that they may fall in love with their Savior;
those in loneliness,
that they may whisper Emmanuel;
those in storms,
that they may stand in awe
of Jesus the storm-breaker. **Amen.**

INVITATION TO OFFERING

The invitation to offering may be led from the Communion table.

God chooses to renew the world
with what you offer from your hands.
What you have in your hands is enough
to overcome evil and feed the world.
Five smooth stones,
five loaves of bread.

Like children who know nothing belongs to them,
who are eager to share and who believe
that what they have is more than enough,
we open our hands, childlike,
before our Father and Mother God.

INVITATION TO THE TABLE

The invitation to the table is led from the Communion table.

Are you wearied and worn,
tired from the work of resistance?
You've done a good job—
not perfect,
but God only needed your willingness.
Be nourished.
Be fed at the true King's table.
Be renewed.

At this table
your sorrow will become rejoicing
and your poverty will make you rich.
At this table
your emptiness will become openness
for everything God can do.

CHARGE

The blessing and charge may be led from the doors of the church.

You are armored not with violence
but with the patience of love,
passion for peace,
and commitment to *shalom* for everyone.
You are stronger than you thought
and meeker than you thought.
This is God's anointing:
Go! And working side by side with Christ,
restore wholeness to the world.
Amen. *or* **Thanks be to God.**

Proper 7

Sunday, June 19–25, if after Trinity Sunday

COMPLEMENTARY READINGS

Job 38:1–11	2 Corinthians 6:1–13
Psalm 107:1–3, 23–32	Mark 4:35–41

OPENING SENTENCES

Give thanks to the Lord, for God is good!
God's steadfast love endures forever.

God's love is boundless.
**The Lord saved us from trouble
and lifted us from our distress.**

Give thanks to the Lord, for God is good!
God's steadfast love endures forever.

PRAYER OF THE DAY

Holy God,
you made the seas and shaped the land;
you set the planets spinning
and scattered the stars throughout the skies.
Even when the earth shakes
and the oceans roar,
you remain steadfast,
calming our fears and quieting our storms.
All thanks and praise to you, O God,
now and forever. **Amen.**

---

*"Where were you when I laid the foundations of
the earth? Tell me, if you have understanding. Who
determined its measurements—surely you know!
Or who stretched the line upon it?"*

Job 38:4–5

INVITATION TO DISCIPLESHIP

The invitation to discipleship may be led from the baptismal font.

In a world full of confusion and pain,
Jesus Christ invites us to walk with him,
that we might follow where he leads
and enter the joy of his kingdom.

If you would follow him,
for the first time or the thousandth,
come, for he waits in love.

PRAYERS OF INTERCESSION

The prayers of intercession may be led from the midst of the congregation.

Almighty God,
though the world is in turmoil,
you are steadfast.
With confidence in your loving care,
we bring our prayers to you.

For those who suffer from natural disasters,
those whose lives are shattered,
those who grieve,
those who provide comfort, water, and food,
and those who rebuild:
God of might, **hear our prayers.**

For polluted skies and unsafe water,
smog-filled air and children with asthma,
fish that die from chemicals,
and waterfowl slicked with oil;
for overfarmed land, clear-cut mountains,
and the loss of old-growth forests:
God of might, **hear our prayers.**

For those who are ill,
those who live with chronic pain,
those suffering diseases,
those undergoing treatments,
and those for whom there is no cure;
for all those who offer healing hands
and kind hearts:
God of might, **hear our prayers.**

For those who suffer in mind or spirit,
those in depression
and those living with anxiety,
those who bear their pain silently
and those who have lost hope,
those lost in addiction
and those seeking sobriety each day:
God of might, **hear our prayers.**

For the deep concerns of our hearts:
[Allow time for silent prayer.]
God of might, **hear our prayer.**

For the gift of prayer
and your promise to hear,
we give you thanks, O God,
trusting all of our lives to you.
In Jesus' name we pray. **Amen.**

INVITATION TO OFFERING

The invitation to offering may be led from the Communion table.

God has done wonderful things for us.

With thanksgiving for the steadfast love of God,
let us bring our tithes and offerings.

INVITATION TO THE TABLE

The invitation to the table is led from the Communion table.

> Come to the table,
> all you who fear,
> for here you will find rest.
> Come to the table,
> you who hunger for Christ,
> for here you will be fed.
> Come to the table,
> you who yearn for the coming of justice
> and the reign of peace,
> for Christ is on his way!
>
> Here is the feast Christ has prepared,
> a sign of the realm to come.

CHARGE

The blessing and charge may be led from the doors of the church.

> Do not be afraid,
> for you do not go alone;
> you are sheltered by the power of God.
> **Amen.** *or* **Thanks be to God.**

Proper 8

Sunday, June 26—July 2

SEMICONTINUOUS READINGS

2 Samuel 1:1, 17–27   2 Corinthians 8:7–15
Psalm 130   Mark 5:21–43

OPENING SENTENCES

My soul waits for God,
like those watching for the morning.
**God brings warmth
and light into our world.**

God's love is steadfast as the sun,
always rising, despite our evening struggles.
**God wakes us up each day
with the gracious gift of new life.**

PRAYER OF THE DAY

Creator, breath of every living thing,
you imagined the world;
you spoke, and it was so.
Jesus, overcomer of death,
you returned to us, your loved ones,
and you promise that one day
we will return to our loved ones.
Spirit, promise-keeper,
at the right time death will end
and the world will be restored
with abundant and eternal life.
This is our hope and prayer. **Amen.**

INVITATION TO DISCIPLESHIP

The invitation to discipleship may be led from the baptismal font.

Jesus takes us into
places of death and despair.
We are there to witness God
doing amazing, life-giving work,
and we get to be partners in that work.
What a beautiful opportunity
to join Jesus
and to be like Jesus.

Come and join this dance of life
we call discipleship.
We will stand by the grace of Jesus.
We will be led by the Holy Spirit.

PRAYERS OF INTERCESSION

The prayers of intercession may be led from the midst of the congregation.

We are people of resurrection.
There is no place or person beyond redemption,
including us.
So we turn to God in prayer.

We lift up the church,
that we would comfort those
who have lost loved ones
to the death that is part of nature;
that we would protest and resist
death that is unnatural.

We lift up the nations,
and people stuck in the belief
that countries and nations are essential identities.
Teach us that our primary identity
is that we are all your people,
living on one planet, needing each other.

We lift up our earth,
the only home we have in this vast universe.
Forgive us for the ways we are ruining it.
Grant us the power of resurrection—
to work together with generosity
and to share our resources with all,
so the earth, your good creation, can renew itself.

This we pray in Jesus' name. **Amen.**

INVITATION TO OFFERING

The invitation to offering may be led from the Communion table.

Remember all the times
God stopped death in its tracks.
Remember all the times
God has given us back what we lost.

God's generous Spirit
inspires the generosity of our hearts.
Let us release the flow of generosity.

INVITATION TO THE TABLE

The invitation to the table is led from the Communion table.

At the Lord's table
we remember the Last Supper,
but we also have a foretaste
of the heavenly feast that is to come.
This table is about the sacrifice of Jesus
but also the return of Jesus.

This is the party before the party,
that great banquet
when we will all sit with Jesus,
all of us healed and whole.
This is a resurrection meal!

CHARGE

The blessing and charge may be led from the doors of the church.

As people filled up with the Spirit of God,
we have the power of creation at our fingertips.
We have words,
words that can give light or make darkness.
So let's speak life.
Our words can bring bones back to life—
even our bones, once broken and brittle.
Love is not impossible.
Nothing is impossible
for us who are brimming with God.
Amen. *or* **Thanks be to God.**

Proper 8

Sunday, June 26—July 2

COMPLEMENTARY READINGS

Wisdom 1:13–15; 2:23–24 *or*   2 Corinthians 8:7–15
  Lamentations 3:22–33   Mark 5:21–43
Psalm 30

OPENING SENTENCES

> The steadfast love of the Lord never ceases;
> **God's mercies never come to an end.**
>
> God's faithfulness is great;
> **our hope is in the Lord.**

PRAYER OF THE DAY

> Great is your faithfulness, O God;
> how we rejoice in you!
> You meet us in our sorrow
> and raise us up in joy.
> You hear our cries for help
> and come to heal and save us.
> Even in death
> you raise us to new life.
> All thanks and praise to you, O God,
> now and forevermore. **Amen.**

For you know the generous act of our Lord Jesus Christ, that though he was rich, yet for your sakes he became poor, so that by his poverty you might become rich.

2 Corinthians 8:9

INVITATION TO DISCIPLESHIP

The invitation to discipleship may be led from the baptismal font.

> Christ waits for whoever seeks him;
> God is ready to welcome you
> with embracing love.
>
> If you yearn for mercy
> or seek God's healing,
> if you wish to belong
> to the company of grace,
> come, for the Lord of life awaits.

PRAYERS OF INTERCESSION

The prayers of intercession may be led from the midst of the congregation.

> Merciful God,
> you comfort all who seek you
> and never waver
> in your loving care for us.
> With thanks and in hope
> we offer our prayers to you.
>
> Heal your aching world, O God.
> Replace our fears of one another
> with understanding and love,
> that wars may stop,
> injustices may cease,
> and your people may live in peace.
> Merciful God, **hear our prayer.**
>
> Renew your wounded earth, O God.
> Refresh our waters, enrich our land,
> and clear our skies,
> that all your creatures may flourish.
> Let the health of the planet be paramount
> for corporations and governments;
> may we all see the beauty and awe
> of this world you have made.
> Merciful God, **hear our prayer.**

Embolden your church, O God.
Fan the flames of our passion for justice,
deepen our desire for peace,
and equip us to witness to your great love.
Merciful God, **hear our prayer.**

Soothe the suffering of all who are ill,
and receive in peace those who are dying.
Strengthen caretakers and give them rest.
Make us ever grateful
for all the ways you heal.
Merciful God, **hear our prayer.**

Uphold your children
who are persecuted or abused
for the color of their skin,
the sound of their accents,
their gender identity,
or their physical difference.
Nurture in us all deep kindness,
and teach us to see with the eyes of love.
Merciful God, **hear our prayer.**

Hear now our silent intercessions . . .
Merciful God, **hear our prayer.**

For everything that has been
and everything that will be,
we give you thanks, O God,
sure of your steadfast love.
In Jesus' name we pray. **Amen.**

INVITATION TO OFFERING

The invitation to offering may be led from the Communion table.

God has turned our mourning into dancing.

Let us bring our gifts
of thanks and praise to God!

INVITATION TO THE TABLE

The invitation to the table is led from the Communion table.

Come to the table,
whether you are weary or glad,
in turmoil or at peace.

If you would see Jesus, come,
for he waits to share this feast
that he has prepared.

CHARGE

The blessing and charge may be led from the doors of the church.

Your faith has made you well.
Go in peace; be healed
and be a source of healing in our world.
Amen. *or* **Thanks be to God.**

Proper 9

Sunday, July 3–9

SEMICONTINUOUS READINGS

2 Samuel 5:1–5, 9–10   2 Corinthians 12:2–10
Psalm 48   Mark 6:1–13

OPENING SENTENCES

Great is the Lord and greatly to be praised
in the city of our God.
God's holy mountain, beautiful in elevation,
is the joy of all the earth.

We ponder your steadfast love, O God,
in the midst of your temple.
Your name, O God, like your praise,
reaches to the ends of the earth.

Walk about Zion, go all around it, count its towers,
that you may tell the next generation that this is God,
our God forever and ever.
God will be our guide forever.

PRAYER OF THE DAY

O Lord, God of hosts,
our constant companion and sure defense,
be pleased to dwell with us this day,
to receive our worship and our praise,
and to truly transform our lives,
that when we are sent out
we may carry with us
only your sufficient grace and perfect power,
as we proclaim your healing love
for the sake of Christ our Lord. **Amen.**

INVITATION TO DISCIPLESHIP

The invitation to discipleship may be led from the baptismal font.

> Whatever you have experienced,
> God's grace is sufficient for you.
>
> Shake from your feet the dust of rejection,
> and find welcome here,
> that together we may embrace
> the ever-expanding realm of God's love.

PRAYERS OF INTERCESSION

The prayers of intercession may be led from the midst of the congregation.

> Gracious God, as we ponder your steadfast love,
> we remember that this love is not for us alone
> but reaches to the ends of the earth.
> And so we pray:
> With power made perfect in weakness, **hear our prayer.**
>
> Strengthen the witness of your church . . .
> Open us to be ready recipients of your deeds of power,
> that we may boast in nothing apart from your work
> within and through us.
> With power made perfect in weakness, **hear our prayer.**
>
> Forever guide the life of the nations . . .
> Bring together the leaders of this world in humility,
> that they may shepherd your people in truth
> and rule in faithfulness.
> With power made perfect in weakness, **hear our prayer.**
>
> Fill the earth with your grace . . .
> Guide our consideration and care for the work of your hands,
> that beauty and bounty may be preserved
> for all generations.
> With power made perfect in weakness, **hear our prayer.**

Dwell with your people in need . . .
May those who are weak be upheld in your power,
and any who are insulted find in you a sure defense.
May those who are sick be anointed with your healing,
and any who are persecuted rest in your victory.
May those who suffer calamity find in you a stronghold,
and any who know hardship discover your tender mercy.
With power made perfect in weakness, **hear our prayer.**

Held by your steadfast love
and guided forever by your wisdom,
we lift these and all our prayers to you, O Lord. **Amen.**

INVITATION TO OFFERING

The invitation to offering may be led from the Communion table.

We do not boast in our possessions,
for all we have has been given by God.

Let us respond to God's deeds of power,
offering that which we have received
and trusting that God's grace is sufficient
to transform our humble offerings
into blessings that will extend to the ends of the earth.

INVITATION TO THE TABLE

The invitation to the table is led from the Communion table.

In a world where welcome is not readily extended,
Christ welcomes all to gather at his table.
In a world where hardships persist,
Christ nourishes and strengthens us by his grace.
In a world where pride of power looks down upon weakness,
Christ offers his body broken and blood poured out in love.

Come to the table.
Receive Christ's welcome, nourishment, and love.

CHARGE

The blessing and charge may be led from the doors of the church.

The one who gathered us now sends us out,
equipped for every challenge
and strengthened in every weakness.
As you go, wherever people will hear you,
proclaim the all-sufficient grace
and perfect power of our God.
Amen. *or* **Thanks be to God.**

Proper 9

Sunday, July 3–9

COMPLEMENTARY READINGS

Ezekiel 2:1–5   2 Corinthians 12:2–10
Psalm 123   Mark 6:1–13

OPENING SENTENCES

In days of joy and tenderness,
we lift up our eyes, seeking you.

In days of anger and frustration,
we lift up our eyes, seeking you.

When we suffer injustice and oppression,
we lift up our eyes, seeking you.

When we sing and clap with joy,
we lift up our eyes, seeking you,
knowing you are there,
O ruler of the heavens.

PRAYER OF THE DAY

O God of the Sabbath, speak to us
even when we are hardheaded and hard-hearted,
even if we have rebelled against you,
even if we refuse to hear.
Speak to us so we can stand up on our feet
and proclaim your Word
through word and deed. **Amen.**

INVITATION TO DISCIPLESHIP

The invitation to discipleship may be led from the baptismal font.

Jesus called disciples from all walks of life,
gathered them,
and sent them to proclaim the good news,
taking nothing for their journey.

Now Christ is calling us.
With the confidence that Christ will give us the words
and the authority to share God's love with the world,
let us begin our journey.

PRAYERS OF INTERCESSION

The prayers of intercession may be led from the midst of the congregation.

Word made flesh,
we come with prayers of gratitude—

for voices that bring healing . . .

for voices that bring comfort . . .

for voices that bring peace . . .

for voices that sing songs
and recite poetry . . .

for the voices of
[name those for whom you are grateful] . . .

We also bring our prayers—

for voices silenced . . .

for voices unheard and ignored . . .

for voices of those who are persecuted . . .

for voices that make us uncomfortable . . .

for voices that speak hard truths . . .

for voices that call us out
while seeking to draw us closer to you . . .

for the voices of
*[name those who are experiencing persecution,
oppression, or alienation]* . . .

May we listen to the voices
of prophets near and far
and become voices of justice and love
everywhere we go. **Amen.**

INVITATION TO OFFERING

The invitation to offering may be led from the Communion table.

Let us bring our gifts, big or small,
to provide for those
who bring nothing for the journey—
no bread,
no bag,
no money on their belts—
for they are God's prophets.

INVITATION TO THE TABLE

The invitation to the table is led from the Communion table.

Knowing we bring nothing for the journey,
Christ has prepared an abundant feast for us,
a safe place for us to rest and recharge,
and a community to call home.

Let us come to the feast
ready to receive these gifts.

CHARGE

The blessing and charge may be led from the doors of the church.

Go and listen to the voices of prophets near and far.
Be prophets and speak truth wherever you see injustice,
for God will put the right words in your mouth.
Amen. *or* **Thanks be to God.**

Proper 10

Sunday, July 10–16

SEMICONTINUOUS READINGS

2 Samuel 6:1–5, 12b–19	Ephesians 1:3–14
Psalm 24	Mark 6:14–29

OPENING SENTENCES

The earth is the Lord's and all that is in it,
the world, and those who live in it;
for God has founded it on the seas,
and established it on the rivers.

Who shall ascend the hill of the Lord?
And who shall stand in God's holy place?
Those who have clean hands and pure hearts,
who do not lift up their souls to what is false
and do not swear deceitfully.

They will receive blessing from the Lord
and vindication from the God of their salvation.
Such is the company of those who seek the Lord,
who seek the face of the God of Jacob.

PRAYER OF THE DAY

God of all wisdom and insight,
as we are gathered in your presence,
make known to us the mystery of your will
and accomplish in us your purposes,
that with clean hands and pure hearts
we may live for the praise of Christ's glory. **Amen.**

INVITATION TO DISCIPLESHIP

The invitation to discipleship may be led from the baptismal font.

God chose us in Christ before the foundation of the world
to be holy and blameless before God in love,
destined for adoption as God's children.

Joining in the company of those who seek the Lord,
let us set our hope on Christ,
choosing to dance before the Lord with all our might
rather than for the powers of this world;
to lift not our souls to what is false
but to rejoice in God's word of truth.

PRAYERS OF INTERCESSION

The prayers of intercession may be led from the midst of the congregation.

King of glory, source of grace,
even as we rejoice in your presence
we bring to you the sorrows of this world.

We lift to you the earth . . .
Free us from selfish whims,
that we may care well for your creation
and see that the abundance it yields
may be distributed justly among all people.
Lord, hear our prayer,
as we set our hope on Christ.

We lift to you the nations of this world . . .
Free us from needless violence
driven by greed or jealousy or fear,
that peoples may live together in safety and peace.
Be with all in positions of authority,
that they may be guided by your wisdom
and that they may protect the vulnerable.
Lord, hear our prayer,
as we set our hope on Christ.

We lift to you the church . . .
Free us to live in righteousness and holiness,
that with courage we may speak truth to power.
Grant perseverance and hope
to any who face danger because of their faith,
and strengthen your people's witness
to your gifts of forgiveness and redemption.
Lord, hear our prayer,
as we set our hope on Christ.

We lift to you our loved ones . . .
Free us to tend to the well-being of one another,
that together we may receive blessing from you, our Lord.
Bring solace to any who feel disregarded or despised
by communities or political agendas.
Uphold those weighed down by grief,
and bring healing to those plagued by illness.
Lord, hear our prayer,
as we set our hope on Christ.

Receive our prayers, O God,
according to your counsel and will,
that as we set our hope on Christ
we might live for the praise of his glory,
until all things in heaven and on earth
are gathered by your love and grace. **Amen.**

INVITATION TO OFFERING

The invitation to offering may be led from the Communion table.

Having received from the Lord,
let us bless God's people with our offerings of well-being
as we seek the wholeness and peace
into which Christ is gathering all creation.

INVITATION TO THE TABLE

The invitation to the table is led from the Communion table.

David gathered all the chosen men of Israel
to rejoice in the presence of the Lord
carried in the ark of God.

Here, Christ gathers us with all people
to rejoice in the presence of the Lord in bread and cup,
carried in the hearts of the community of God.

Come, receive this foretaste of the fullness of time
when all things in heaven and on earth
will be gathered up in Christ.

CHARGE

The blessing and charge may be led from the doors of the church.

Having celebrated God's presence here
in the Word proclaimed
and in bread and cup shared among us,
go back to your homes to seek the Lord in all places,
that your life may be an offering of well-being for all people.
Amen. *or* **Thanks be to God.**

Proper 10

Sunday, July 10–16

COMPLEMENTARY READINGS

Amos 7:7–15   Ephesians 1:3–14
Psalm 85:8–13   Mark 6:14–29

OPENING SENTENCES

Because peace is making a road for our steps,
¡venimos a escuchar lo que dice nuestro Dios!
(we come to listen to what our God is saying!)

Because truth is springing up from the ground,
¡venimos a escuchar lo que dice nuestro Dios!
(we come to listen to what our God is saying!)

Because God's salvation is very near,
¡venimos a escuchar lo que dice nuestro Dios!
(we come to listen to what our God is saying!)

Let us rejoice,
for faithful love and truth have met;
righteousness and peace have kissed.
God is in our midst!

PRAYER OF THE DAY

O God who speaks to the people
through voices of yesterday and today,
bring your word for us.
Speak through shepherds and farmworkers,
through tree trimmers and landscapers,
through those who work the land
you love so much.
For they know the pain of the earth,
the pain of the people,
what needs to be done,
and what hope can create.
Give us open hearts to listen to their message
and open hands to do the work you ask of us. **Amen.**

INVITATION TO DISCIPLESHIP

The invitation to discipleship may be led from the baptismal font.

The Holy One called Amos, an ordinary human,
to prophesy to God's people.
In the same way,
the Holy One is calling us, ordinary people,
to speak up and spread God's message to the world.

Let us gladly accept this invitation
to live prophetic lives.

PRAYERS OF INTERCESSION

The prayers of intercession may be led from the midst of the congregation.

For choosing us to be your people,
loving us before the creation of the world,
and adopting us all to be your children,
we give you thanks,
loving Parent of us all.

For forgiving our trespasses,
pouring out your overflowing grace,
and revealing your hidden design to us,
we give you thanks,
loving Parent of us all.

For those who feel rejected,
those who have felt unloved since they were born,
those who have been abandoned by their families,
we lift our prayers,
loving Parent of us all.

For those trespasses we can't forget,
the hatred we encounter in the world,
and the lies we hear in the news,
we lift our prayers,
loving Parent of us all.

We pray these things with the confidence
that in the fullness of time
you will gather up all things
into your loving embrace—
all things in heaven and on earth. **Amen.**

INVITATION TO OFFERING

The invitation to offering may be led from the Communion table.

We are called to bring honor to God's glory.

So let us bring our whole selves—
our gifts of time, prayer, and resources—
to do the work of bringing good news
to all of God's children.

INVITATION TO THE TABLE

The invitation to the table is led from the Communion table.

The one who has called us beloved children
has prepared a table for us.

Let us gather everyone
and feast together as a family.

CHARGE

The blessing and charge may be led from the doors of the church.

Go out to this world
and embrace everyone you encounter,
for every face you see
is the face of one of God's children.
Amen. *or* **Thanks be to God.**

Proper 11

Sunday, July 17–23

SEMICONTINUOUS READINGS

2 Samuel 7:1–14a	Ephesians 2:11–22
Psalm 89:20–37	Mark 6:30–34, 53–56

OPENING SENTENCES

In Christ, you who once were far off
have been brought near by the blood of Christ,
for he is our peace.

In Christ we are no longer strangers;
we are members of the household of God.

We are built upon the foundation of the apostles and prophets
with Christ Jesus as the cornerstone.

In Christ we are built together spiritually
into a dwelling place for God.
Let us worship God, in whom we all dwell.

PRAYER OF THE DAY

All-gracious God, Rock of our salvation,
you have drawn us near
to rest a while in your sure and solid presence.
As you meet us here,
filled with compassion,
ready to receive our prayers and our praise,
so fill us with compassion
that we may follow wherever you go,
ready to receive all who are in need.
Through your Son Jesus Christ,
the cornerstone of our faith. **Amen.**

INVITATION TO DISCIPLESHIP

The invitation to discipleship may be led from the baptismal font.

As a structure must be built upon a solid foundation,
so this community is built upon the presence of Christ.
Walls that divide are not found here,
but only the materials of life abundant:
peace and justice, love and compassion.

Let us find our home in Christ,
even as Christ makes his home in us.
Then let us follow to the places where life is threatened,
ever oriented to Christ, our cornerstone.

PRAYERS OF INTERCESSION

The prayers of intercession may be led from the midst of the congregation.

God of all,
we give thanks that you are ever with us,
and we remember that you are also with those
on the other side of every dividing wall.
And so we pray not only for ourselves
but for all those with whom we are joined
into a dwelling place for you.

Gathering God,
we bring to you those who wander
like sheep without a shepherd
and those who long to touch the fringe of your cloak,
trusting that you choose not to dwell
solely in the comfort of our homes
or the safety of our sanctuaries
but in every place where your people may be found.

Healing God,
we bring to you those who are sick
and those who care for them,
trusting that you choose to pace hospital hallways,
tenderly holding the hands of worried and wearied souls
awaiting news of loved ones.

Restoring God,
we bring to you those whose hearts are filled with fear
in countries torn apart by war,
and those whose homes are devastated
by water, wind, or flame,
trusting that you choose to build hope
in the rubble of disaster and destruction.

Redeeming God,
we bring to you those pushed to the fringes of society
who long for a place of belonging,
families separated by national borders,
and people weighed down by oppressive powers,
trusting that you choose to be heard
in the voices that cry out for justice.

God of all compassion,
we bring to you these and all our prayers,
trusting that you already promise that for which we ask.
Tear down the walls we construct to make us feel protected,
and set your church ever on the move,
that we might discover you at work in all places
and discover ourselves as members of your household.
Through Christ our Lord. **Amen.**

INVITATION TO OFFERING

The invitation to offering may be led from the Communion table.

We offer our very best to the honor and glory of God,
because we trust that God knows better
the needed materials for the building of God's kingdom.

Therefore let us give of ourselves—
to the breaking down of dividing walls
and the building up of peace.

INVITATION TO THE TABLE

The invitation to the table is led from the Communion table.

Here we discover in ordinary bread and cup
a dwelling place for our Lord.
Here we are joined one to another,
built together spiritually into a dwelling place for God.

The Lord who meets us here
promises to be with us wherever we may go.

CHARGE

The blessing and charge may be led from the doors of the church.

Having rested a while in the presence of the Lord this day,
go forth to discover Christ at work wherever there is need,
proclaiming peace to all, far and near.
Return here in due time to rest in the Lord yet again,
knowing that those who see you coming and going
will recognize Christ at work through you.
Amen. *or* **Thanks be to God.**

Proper 11

Sunday, July 17–23

COMPLEMENTARY READINGS

Jeremiah 23:1–6   Ephesians 2:11–22
Psalm 23   Mark 6:30–34, 53–56

OPENING SENTENCES

Green pastures and still waters
¡son obra del Buen Pastor!
(are the work of the Good Shepherd!)

Flocks to belong to and safe pathways
¡son obra del Buen Pastor!
(are the work of the Good Shepherd!)

Bountiful tables and anointing oil
¡son obra del Buen Pastor!
(are the work of the Good Shepherd!)

We come with songs and praises
for the Good Shepherd who has brought us here.
Let us worship God!

PRAYER OF THE DAY

We gather around you, O Jesus,
to tell you what we have done.
And you say to us,
"Come and rest a while."
So we give you thanks
for this time of rest and reflection.
In this sacred time, prepare us
for the work ahead of us. **Amen.**

INVITATION TO DISCIPLESHIP

The invitation to discipleship may be led from the baptismal font.

Christ has given us citizenship
in the kin-dom* of God.
Let us proclaim Christ's peace
to those who are far off
and to those who are near.
Let us reconcile with our siblings
and break down any hostility
we have with one another.

PRAYERS OF INTERCESSION

The prayers of intercession may be led from the midst of the congregation.

O Good Shepherd,
we come today with prayers
for the sheep of your pasture:

[after each sentence you may name specific people or groups]

for those who have been destroyed and scattered . . .

for those who have been driven away . . .

for those who cannot lie down and rest . . .

for those who thirst and hunger . . .

for those who have no hope . . .

for those walking through the valley of the shadow of death . . .

for those who are still seen as strangers and aliens . . .

But we also pray for your other flock:

for those who have not attended to your sheep . . .

---

*The term *kin-dom* of God was originally coined by mujerista theologian Ada María Isasi-Díaz to indicate we are all part of God's family.

for those who have driven other sheep away . . .

for those who take away food and drink . . .

for those who have built a dividing wall . . .

We pray that you reconcile both groups to you in one body,
to journey together as one flock,
for you are indeed
our Good Shepherd. **Amen.**

INVITATION TO OFFERING

The invitation to offering may be led from the Communion table.

In Christ we are no longer strangers and aliens,
but members of the household of God.

With joy and gratitude
let us bring our gifts,
so the table God has spread
can feed all the sheep of God's flock.

INVITATION TO THE TABLE

The invitation to the table is led from the Communion table.

Our shepherd,
the one who has gathered us in this place,
has spread a table before us,
knowing that we need sustenance for the journey ahead.

Let us follow the Good Shepherd
and rejoice in this meal!

CHARGE

The blessing and charge may be led from the doors of the church.

Now go and gather all the sheep
that have been scattered,
and share with them this good news:
Do not fear or be dismayed,
for God has raised up shepherds to care for you.
Amen. *or* **Thanks be to God.**

Proper 12

Sunday, July 24–30

SEMICONTINUOUS READINGS

2 Samuel 11:1–15   Ephesians 3:14–21
Psalm 14   John 6:1–21

OPENING SENTENCES

The Lord looks down from heaven on humankind
to see if there are any who are wise,
who seek after God.
**Strengthened with power through the Spirit,
may we seek to know the love of Christ
that surpasses knowledge.**

PRAYER OF THE DAY

God of abundance,
we are empty and long to be filled;
we are hungry and long to be fed;
we are lost and long to be found.
As you gather us in your presence,
gather the fragments of our broken lives,
that even in our scarcity
the abundance of your grace
may show forth. **Amen.**

---

*The LORD looks down from heaven on humankind to see
if there are any who are wise, who seek after God. They
have all gone astray, they are all alike perverse; there is
no one who does good, no, not one.*

Psalm 14:2–3

INVITATION TO DISCIPLESHIP

The invitation to discipleship may be led from the baptismal font.

In a world that questions whether there is enough,
God shows us that in the community of Christ
all we have and all we are is more than enough.

Complete belief is not a prerequisite
to be a part of this community.
Wisdom is found
not in unquestioned assurance
or blind faith,
but in seeking after God.

You are ever welcome, ever invited,
to seek God alongside this community,
that together we may be filled with all the fullness of God.

PRAYERS OF INTERCESSION

The prayers of intercession may be led from the midst of the congregation.

We bow our knees before you, Holy Father,
from whom every family in heaven and on earth
takes its name,
trusting that you hear us when we call upon you.

We pray for the world . . .
Grant wisdom to those who govern,
free them from corruption,
and equip them for the work they are called to do.
Be a refuge to the poor and vulnerable,
root out the causes of injustice
and inequitable distribution of resources.
Have mercy upon those swept up
by strong winds of violence or prejudice,
displacement or terror.
Gather all the peoples of the nations
to sit down together in peace,
recognizing our common need.

We pray for the church . . .
Grant wisdom to your people,
that we might truly seek after you
and share the blessings of Christ freely.
Be with those who have gone astray,
and gather them into your presence
that none may be lost.
Reveal to us the provision you supply,
and open us to every invitation
to participate in the signs of your kingdom.
Dwell in our hearts through faith,
that we may be rooted and grounded in love.

We pray for loved ones . . .
Grant wisdom to those who are struggling,
and strengthen them in your love,
that they may trust in you.
Restore to health those who suffer
in body, mind, or spirit.
Fill those who hunger,
and assure those who doubt.
Deliver those who have been deeply betrayed
by the deeds of others.
Come to those tossed about by the rough sea of anxiety,
and speak comfort to those who are afraid.

With these and all the prayers of our hearts
we call upon you, O Lord,
until, by your word and outstretched arms,
this world reaches the place toward which it is going—
the land of your eternal presence. **Amen.**

INVITATION TO OFFERING

The invitation to offering may be led from the Communion table.

On behalf of a brokenhearted world,
let us offer even our humble gifts
to the God who gathers up the broken pieces
and feeds a multitude.

INVITATION TO THE TABLE

The invitation to the table is led from the Communion table.

One loaf and one cup—
what are they among so many people?

The one who fed the crowds
with merely five loaves and two fish,
then gathered up the leftovers,
gathers us at this table to discover
the breadth and length and height and depth
of a love that surpasses knowledge.

CHARGE

The blessing and charge may be led from the doors of the church.

Go from here to seek after God,
who by the power at work within us
is able to accomplish abundantly far more
than all we can ask or imagine.
Amen. *or* **Thanks be to God.**

Proper 12

Sunday, July 24–30

COMPLEMENTARY READINGS

2 Kings 4:42–44   Ephesians 3:14–21
Psalm 145:10–18   John 6:1–21

OPENING SENTENCES

For the trustworthiness of your words,
all creation gives thanks to you, O God!

For your closeness to those who call out to you,
all creation gives thanks to you, O God!

For your support of those who fall down,
all creation gives thanks to you, O God!

For your providential care,
satisfying the needs of every living creature,
all creation gives thanks to you, O God!
Let us praise the Maker of the universe!

PRAYER OF THE DAY

With barley loaves
and sacks of grain,
with prayers of thanksgiving
and pleas for help,
O God, we come to you today—
to be fed,
to get rest,
to be transformed,
to be sent out,
to feed the world. **Amen.**

INVITATION TO DISCIPLESHIP

The invitation to discipleship may be led from the baptismal font.

In the vastness of the night,
in the power of the storm,
in the terror of the unknown,
Christ met the disciples and said to them,
"It is I; do not be afraid."

In the same way,
Christ is meeting us, right here and now,
inviting us to jump into the breadth and length
and height and depth of God's love.
Do not be afraid.
Christ is with us.

PRAYERS OF INTERCESSION

The prayers of intercession may be led from the midst of the congregation.

We come with words of praise,
for you are faithful and merciful
and you open your hands
to feed every creature in due season.
For all the blessings that come from you,
O Creator of wheat and yeast,
we give you thanks.

We come with heavy hearts,
for we witness injustice and war,
we suffer anxiety and loneliness,
and we participate in systems that oppress others.
For all the pain in the world,
O God who is near,
we call upon your name.

We come with hopes and dreams
of families reunited,
of relationships restored,
of peace reigning on earth.
For all who are cast down,
O God who makes us whole,
we lift up our prayers today. Amen.

INVITATION TO OFFERING

The invitation to offering may be led from the Communion table.

When we share what we have,
no matter how much or how little,
God uses it to satisfy the needs
of every living creature.

Let us bring our loaves and fishes,
every gift we have,
so we can witness the miracle
of God's community in action.

INVITATION TO THE TABLE

The invitation to the table is led from the Communion table.

Simple gifts, loaves and fishes,
can feed thousands.
Simple gifts, loaves and fishes,
can teach the world about the power of sharing.
Simple gifts, loaves and fishes,
can change the course of history.

All are invited—
to share, to eat, to gather crumbs,
to see the extraordinary
in the most ordinary of activities:
sharing a meal.

CHARGE

The blessing and charge may be led from the doors of the church.

The one who has fed us calls us out—
to gather crumbs and feed the world.
Amen. *or* **Thanks be to God.**

Proper 13

Sunday, July 31—August 6

SEMICONTINUOUS READINGS

2 Samuel 11:26–12:13a   Ephesians 4:1–16
Psalm 51:1–12   John 6:24–35

OPENING SENTENCES

> God desires truth in the inward being.
> **Therefore teach me wisdom in my secret heart.**
>
> God purges with hyssop, that we shall all be clean.
> **Wash me, and I shall be whiter than snow.**
>
> Create in me a clean heart, O God,
> **and put a new and right spirit within me.**
>
> Do not cast me away from your presence,
> **and do not take your Holy Spirit from me.**
>
> Restore to me the joy of your salvation,
> **and sustain in me a willing spirit.**

PRAYER OF THE DAY

> Gracious God,
> the eyes of all look to you in hope;
> you open your hand
> and satisfy the hunger and thirst of every living thing.
> Satisfy our hunger through Christ, the bread of life,
> and quench our thirst with the gift of belief,
> that we may no longer work for food that perishes
> but receive that which endures for eternal life,
> even Jesus Christ our Lord. **Amen.**

INVITATION TO DISCIPLESHIP

The invitation to discipleship may be led from the baptismal font.

There is one body and one Spirit,
just as you were called to the one hope of your calling—
one Lord, one faith, one baptism,
one God and Parent of us all,
who is above all and through all and in all.

Though we seem so often to be tossed to and fro,
blown about by every wind except that of God's Spirit,
the Lord gathers us to lead a life worthy of our calling,
with all humility and gentleness, with patience,
bearing with one another in love,
making every effort to maintain the unity of the Spirit
in the bond of peace.

For it is in that unity that we are equipped
to grow up in every way into him who is the head,
from whom we, Christ's body,
are joined and knitted together.
You are a part of this body.
Join us as we seek to grow in love.

PRAYERS OF INTERCESSION

The prayers of intercession may be led from the midst of the congregation.

God of all goodness and grace,
you desire truth in the inward being.
Search our hearts as we seek after you,
and receive our prayers in your mercy and love.

Have mercy upon this world, O God . . .
We pray for leaders and those in positions of power,
that they may be guided by your truth
and attentive to the needs of your people.
We pray for those whose voices have been silenced,
those unjustly separated from loved ones,
and those who are hungry, homeless, or hopeless.

Have mercy upon your church, O God . . .
We pray for those who are seeking
yet know not that for which they seek.
We pray that you would make your church
humble, gentle, and patient,
living a life worthy of its calling.
Equip the saints for the work of ministry,
for the building up of the body of Christ.

Have mercy upon our hearts, O God . . .
We pray for those who have heard hard truths
of illness, loss, or disrupted dreams;
for those who have heard false words
of hate or harm, unwelcome or denial.
We pray that you would cleanse our lives
of anything that displeases you,
whether done to us or by us.

By your abundant mercy and steadfast love, O God,
receive our prayers and embolden all people
to recognize and celebrate the gifts of your Spirit
in one another.
Satiate our needs with that which you alone can offer,
and direct our longings toward that which is true.
Through Christ our Lord. **Amen.**

INVITATION TO OFFERING

The invitation to offering may be led from the Communion table.

When he ascended on high,
our Lord Jesus Christ gave gifts to his people.

As grateful recipients, claimed by God's grace,
let us offer these gifts for the ministry of Christ.

INVITATION TO THE TABLE

The invitation to the table is led from the Communion table.

Our Savior said, "I am the bread of life.
Whoever comes to me will never be hungry,
and whoever believes in me will never be thirsty."

Christ invites you and all people to come to his table.
Through the bread broken and the cup shared,
the Lord meets us here with the gift of belief,
that by grace we may grow in love as the body of Christ,
given for the life of the world.

CHARGE

The blessing and charge may be led from the doors of the church.

Gifted by grace, called to love, and equipped with belief,
go forth to build up the body of Christ,
until all people come to the unity of the faith
and the knowledge of the Son of God.
Amen. *or* **Thanks be to God.**

Proper 13

Sunday, July 31—August 6

COMPLEMENTARY READINGS

Exodus 16:2–4, 9–15   Ephesians 4:1–16
Psalm 78:23–29   John 6:24–35

OPENING SENTENCES

How can we keep from praising you
when you rain down bread from heaven—
**when you patiently hear our complaints
and love us, even though we don't trust you?**

How can we keep from singing to you
when you open the doors of heaven—
**when you cause the east wind to blow
and answer our fears with a feast?**

Here we are, to praise you and sing to you!
Let us worship the Bread of Life!

PRAYER OF THE DAY

Source of eternal bread,
we give you thanks.
In the midst of an uncertain journey
you feed us,
you quench our thirst,
you appease our anxious minds.
Speak to our hearts and souls today.
Assure us of your faithfulness,
so we can take the next steps faithfully
as we seek to follow you. **Amen.**

INVITATION TO DISCIPLESHIP

The invitation to discipleship may be led from the baptismal font.

Christ gave a variety of gifts to the people of God,
each unique, each needed, each beloved.

Christ invites us to use our gifts,
joined and knit together by every ligament,
for the service of the whole body
as it grows together, building itself up in love.

PRAYERS OF INTERCESSION

The prayers of intercession may be led from the midst of the congregation.

We come with joyful prayers—
for the life you have given us,
for the gifts you have given us,
for the call you have given us.
**Pan de Vida (Bread of Life),
te damos gracias (we give you thanks).**

We come with sorrowful prayers—
for those who don't have bread,
for those who live in drought,
for those whose gifts go unappreciated.
**Agua Eterna (Eternal Water),
te pedimos por ellos (we pray for them).**

We come with angry prayers—
for lives lost in famine and war,
for wildfires caused by human actions,
for systems that benefit only a few.
**Santo Manna (Holy Manna),
te pedimos valor (we ask for courage).**

We come with hopeful prayers—
for faithful ways to use our gifts,
for building up the body of Christ,
for all of us to come to the unity of faith.
**¡Dios Trino (Triune God),
transfórmanos hoy (transform us today)!**

INVITATION TO OFFERING

The invitation to offering may be led from the Communion table.

When holy manna rained down
on the people of Israel,
the people shared the food
until everyone was fed.

Let us bring what we have to feed the world.

INVITATION TO THE TABLE

The invitation to the table is led from the Communion table.

What is it?
The miracle of this table
sometimes feels like a mystery
impossible to understand.
But the feast is here,
ready to nurture us,
to renew our energy for the journey ahead.

Come, even if you don't understand this mystery.
Holy manna has been served for all of us.

CHARGE

The blessing and charge may be led from the doors of the church.

Now go and walk with God
in a manner worthy of the calling
to which you have been called—
with all humility and gentleness,
with patience,
bearing with one another in love,
making every effort
to maintain the unity of the Spirit
in the bond of peace,
and speaking the truth in love.
Amen. *or* **Thanks be to God.**

Proper 14

Sunday, August 7–13

SEMICONTINUOUS READINGS

2 Samuel 18:5–9, 15, 31–33   Ephesians 4:25–5:2
Psalm 130   John 6:35, 41–51

OPENING SENTENCES

I wait for the Holy One;
my soul waits, and in God's Word I hope.
My soul waits for God,
more than those who watch for the morning.

O people of God, hope in the Holy One!
With God there is steadfast love
and great power to redeem.

PRAYER OF THE DAY

Living God,
feed us until we want no more.
Surrounded as we are by grief and anxiety,
by false words and broken relationships,
we are hungry for your healing presence.
Nourish us with your truth
and comfort us with your compassion,
that we might console our neighbor
and provide for those in need.
This we pray
as we wait upon your steadfast love,
through Jesus Christ, our Lord. **Amen.**

*Your ancestors ate the manna in the wilderness, and they
died. This is the bread that comes down from heaven, so
that one may eat of it and not die.*

John 6:49–50

INVITATION TO DISCIPLESHIP

The invitation to discipleship may be led from the baptismal font.

Through the gift of baptism
we are claimed by the love of God,
redeemed by the grace of Christ,
and marked by the seal of the Spirit.

If you are ready to go deeper—
to receive the sacrament of baptism
or live more fully into the promise of baptism—
we invite you to join this community of faith
in the lifelong journey of discipleship.

PRAYERS OF INTERCESSION

The prayers of intercession may be led from the midst of the congregation.

O Holy One, hear our voices;
attend to us as we pray.

We pray for those who grieve this day,
mourning lost loved ones,
broken relationships,
or abandoned dreams.
O God, we wait with them for your consolation.

We pray for those who hunger this day,
longing for food and shelter,
for companionship,
or for justice.
O God, we wait with them for your provision.

We pray for those who seek truth this day,
looking for answers,
diagnoses,
or closure.
O God, we wait with them for your wisdom.

We pray for all those who wait this day,
who feel lost, forsaken, and insecure;
who are beset by anxiety, worry, and fear;
who cry out to you from the depths,
or who are worn out from their crying.
O God, we wait with them for your presence.

With those who cannot even speak their prayers aloud,
O God, we wait.

With well-worn hope and faithful service,
O God, we wait.

More than those who watch for the morning,
O God, we wait.

Come swiftly to our aid. **Amen.**

INVITATION TO OFFERING

The invitation to offering may be led from the Communion table.

To speak the truth and resist evil,
to work honestly with our own hands,
to share what we have with the needy,
to put away bitterness and wrath,
to be kind, tenderhearted, and forgiving—
this is our sacrifice to God,
a fragrant offering of thanks and praise.

Let us present our lives to the Lord.

INVITATION TO THE TABLE

The invitation to the table is led from the Communion table.

The bread that came down from heaven
dwells among us even now.
This is his table,
where all are invited
and none should go hungry.
At this table, we are made one.

Come. All is prepared.

The blessing and charge may be led from the doors of the church.

Nourished by the one who calls us beloved,
let us leave this gathering,
equipped for active waiting,
for tender accompaniment,
and for relationships abundant with grace.
Amen. *or* **Thanks be to God.**

Proper 14

Sunday, August 7–13

COMPLEMENTARY READINGS

1 Kings 19:4–8   Ephesians 4:25–5:2
Psalm 34:1–8   John 6:35, 41–51

OPENING SENTENCES

> Jesus said, "I am the bread of life."
> **Whoever comes to Christ**
> **will never be hungry,**
> **and whoever believes in Christ**
> **will never thirst.**
>
> Jesus said, "I am the bread of life."
> **Our ancestors ate manna and died,**
> **but this is the bread of heaven;**
> **those who eat of it will never die.**
>
> Jesus said, "I am the bread of life."
> **Jesus is the living bread**
> **that came down from heaven.**
> **Whoever eats of this bread**
> **will live forever.**

PRAYER OF THE DAY

> Lord Jesus Christ,
> you are bread for a hungry world.
> Feed us by your Word
> and fill us with your Spirit,
> that we may believe in you
> and have life in your name. **Amen.**

INVITATION TO DISCIPLESHIP

The invitation to discipleship may be led from the baptismal font.

We are called to be imitators of God—
to live in love as Christ has loved us,
to be a fragrant offering of praise to God.

Are you ready to take up Christ's call
to live in peace and love?
Are you ready to lift up your life
as a sacrifice of praise to God?
Come and join this community of faith
in the journey of discipleship.

PRAYERS OF INTERCESSION

The prayers of intercession may be led from the midst of the congregation.

To you, O Lord, we cry.
Save us from every trouble.
Deliver us from all our fears.
God of grace, **hear our prayer.**

We pray for immigrants and refugees
and all who wander in the wilderness.
Give them strength for their journey
and sanctuary among the faithful.
God of grace, **hear our prayer.**

We pray for peace among neighbors
and all who are divided by hatred.
Build us up as a loving community,
and let our words be filled with grace.
God of grace, **hear our prayer.**

We pray for those who toil for a living
and all who struggle to find work.
Let there be fair wages for honest labor
and enough to share with those in need.
God of grace, **hear our prayer.**

We pray for the sick and sorrowful
and all who have drawn close to death.
Comfort those who are suffering,
and fill us with the life of your Spirit.
God of grace, **hear our prayer.**

O Lord, we bless you at all times;
your praise is always on our lips.
We seek you, and you answer us;
we look to you, and you shine upon us.
Receive the prayers of our hearts,
and strengthen us to serve you;
through Jesus Christ our Savior. **Amen.**

INVITATION TO OFFERING

The invitation to offering may be led from the Communion table.

Jesus is the living bread
who gives his body for the life of the world.

Let us share our daily bread
with Jesus Christ, the bread of life.

INVITATION TO THE TABLE

The invitation to the table is led from the Communion table.

As God provided for the prophet Elijah,
God provides us with nourishment
for our journey through the wilderness.

People of God, come—
taste and see that the Lord is good.

CHARGE

The blessing and charge may be led from the doors of the church.

Go forth in the strength of the Spirit
to share the bread of life with the world.
Amen. *or* **Thanks be to God.**

Proper 15

Sunday, August 14–20

SEMICONTINUOUS READINGS

1 Kings 2:10–12; 3:3–14   Ephesians 5:15–20
Psalm 111   John 6:51–58

OPENING SENTENCES

Praise the Lord!
**I will give thanks to the Lord
with my whole heart,
in the company of the upright,
in the congregation.**

The fear of the Lord
is the beginning of wisdom.
**All those who practice it
have a good understanding.
God's praise endures forever.**

PRAYER OF THE DAY

Living God,
you sent Jesus Christ
to lead us from death to life.
Open our minds to his teaching,
that we may follow him faithfully;
then help us proclaim the gospel,
that all the world may believe.
In Christ's name we pray. **Amen.**

---

*At Gibeon the LORD appeared to Solomon in
a dream by night; and God said, "Ask what I
should give you."*

1 Kings 3:5

INVITATION TO DISCIPLESHIP

The invitation to discipleship may be led from the baptismal font.

Solomon sought God's wisdom—
the ability to discern between good and evil.
Jesus shows us God's way—
the path that leads from death to life.

Are you looking for wisdom?
Are you seeking God's way?
Come and join this community of faith
in the journey of discipleship.

PRAYERS OF INTERCESSION

The prayers of intercession may be led from the midst of the congregation.

O Holy Wisdom,
you know everything that happens,
you hear every shout of joy,
and you hold every tear we cry.
Still, you long to listen our prayers,
so that we can come to understand
that you not only know us,
but also care for us.

For those seeking understanding minds
for situations beyond our comprehension—
long-lasting illnesses,
sudden losses,
devastating disasters—
O God of compassion, we pray.

For those seeking discernment
as they make difficult decisions—
the path forward in a fractured relationship,
the best way to care for a loved one,
the next right step—
O God of compassion, we pray.

For those entrusted with leadership roles,
making choices that impact the lives of others—
in neighborhood and local settings,
state-wide, national, and global organizations—
O God of compassion, we pray.

For all the situations that we will never know—
the lives, loves, and losses
that we can never fully understand,
the people and situations we prefer to ignore—
O God of compassion, we pray.

Grant us, O God,
hearts and minds that seek to understand,
ears and spirits prepared to listen,
and arms and communities equipped to embrace,
every single person that you have made,
through Jesus Christ we pray. **Amen.**

INVITATION TO OFFERING

The invitation to offering may be led from the Communion table.

As we sing psalms and hymns
and spiritual songs to one another,
making melody to God in our hearts,
let us give thanks to God
at all times and for everything—
through our gifts,
our deeds,
our words,
and our lives,
in the name of our Lord Jesus Christ.

Singing thanks, singing praise, singing joy,
let us offer our lives to God.

INVITATION TO THE TABLE

The invitation to the table is led from the Communion table.

Jesus, the living bread,
given for the life of the world,
desires to nourish all gathered here,
not only with abundant food and drink,
but also with wisdom and understanding.
He provides food for those who fear him
and is mindful of his covenant
with those who love him.

All is made ready.
Everyone is welcome.

CHARGE

The blessing and charge may be led from the doors of the church.

Let us be careful, then, how we live,
not as unwise people but as wise,
able to discern between good and evil,
broken and made whole in Jesus Christ
for the life of the world.
Amen. *or* **Thanks be to God.**

Proper 15

Sunday, August 14–20

COMPLEMENTARY READINGS

Proverbs 9:1–6   Ephesians 5:15–20
Psalm 34:9–14   John 6:51–58

OPENING SENTENCES

O worship the Lord, you holy ones;
those who fear God have no want.
Even the young lions suffer hunger,
but those who seek the Lord lack nothing.

Come, O children, and listen to me;
I will teach you to worship the Lord.
We will depart from evil and do good;
we will seek peace and pursue it.

PRAYER OF THE DAY

Lord Jesus Christ,
you are living bread from heaven.
Feed us with your body
and fill us with your blood,
that we may have eternal life
and abide in you always;
in your holy name we pray. **Amen.**

INVITATION TO DISCIPLESHIP

The invitation to discipleship may be led from the baptismal font.

With wisdom God calls us
to make the most of the time—
singing psalms, hymns, and spiritual songs
and giving thanks to God in all things.

Come and join us in the song of faith.
Come and lift up your heart to the Lord.

PRAYERS OF INTERCESSION

The prayers of intercession may be led from the midst of the congregation.

O Lord our God, through Jesus Christ
you have given your life for the world.
Receive our prayers in his name.
God of grace, **hear our prayer.**

We pray for students and teachers
and all who long for wisdom.
Help them to increase in knowledge,
that they may glimpse your glory.
God of grace, **hear our prayer.**

We pray for children and youth
and all who are growing in faith.
Guide them in your way of life,
that they may live to sing your praise.
God of grace, **hear our prayer.**

We pray for this hurting planet
and all who seek to preserve it.
Show us how to care for creation,
that all creatures may find rest in you.
God of grace, **hear our prayer.**

We pray for people who are poor
and all who hunger and thirst.
Satisfy them with your abundance,
that they may want no more.
God of grace, **hear our prayer.**

O Lord our God, through Jesus Christ
you have come to abide in us.
Let us abide in you always,
giving thanks in all things.
In Jesus' name we pray. **Amen.**

INVITATION TO OFFERING

The invitation to offering may be led from the Communion table.

Jesus offers his life for us—
his flesh and blood for the life of the world.

Let us offer our lives to God,
giving thanks for the grace of Christ.

INVITATION TO THE TABLE

The invitation to the table is led from the Communion table.

Wisdom built this house.
Now she calls to us:
"Come, eat of my bread
and drink of the wine I have mixed.
Lay aside immaturity, and live,
and walk in the way of insight."

People of God, come—
taste and see that the Lord is good.

CHARGE

The blessing and charge may be led from the doors of the church.

Be filled with the Spirit,
and give thanks to God
in the name of the Lord Jesus Christ.
Amen. *or* **Thanks be to God.**

Proper 16

Sunday, August 21–27

SEMICONTINUOUS READINGS

1 Kings 8:(1, 6, 10–11) 22–30,   Ephesians 6:10–20
  41–43   John 6:56–69
Psalm 84

OPENING SENTENCES

How lovely is your dwelling place,
O Lord of hosts!
My soul longs and faints
for the courts of the Lord;
my heart and flesh sing with joy
to the living God.

Even the sparrow finds a home
and the swallow a nest
at your altars, O Lord of hosts.
Happy are those
who live in your house,
ever singing your praise.

PRAYER OF THE DAY

Living God,
you sent Jesus Christ
to be your Word made flesh.
Fill us with your Spirit,
that we may believe in him;
send us by your Spirit,
that we may share good news.
In Christ's name we pray. **Amen.**

INVITATION TO DISCIPLESHIP

The invitation to discipleship may be led from the baptismal font.

Through the gift of baptism
we are clothed with grace—
robed with the righteousness of Christ,
wrapped in the mercy of the Lord,
covered by the strength of the Spirit.

You are invited to put on this heavenly garment—
to receive the sacrament of baptism
or to reaffirm your baptismal promises.
We are ready to accompany and support you
in the joyful life of discipleship.

PRAYERS OF INTERCESSION

The prayers of intercession may be led from the midst of the congregation.

O Lord of hosts, you alone are holy.
Hear the prayers of your people:

for the earth that is our home . . .

for churches around the world . . .

for the people of this nation . . .

for the people of all nations . . .

for those seeking sanctuary . . .

for those who are in prison . . .

for those who are hungry . . .

for those who are alone . . .

for teachers and students . . .

for friends and loved ones . . .

O Lord, you are our sun and shield.
Bestow your favor and honor upon us,
that we may receive all good things
and share them with those in need;
through Jesus Christ our Savior. **Amen.**

INVITATION TO OFFERING

The invitation to offering may be led from the Communion table.

There is no God like the Lord
in heaven above or on earth below,
keeping covenant and steadfast love forever.

With awe and wonder,
with love and rejoicing,
with gratitude and praise,
let us offer our lives to the Lord.

INVITATION TO THE TABLE

The invitation to the table is led from the Communion table.

Happy are those who come to this table.
When we share this meal with Jesus,
through the power of the Holy Spirit,
we abide in Christ, and Christ abides in us.

Come and find rest at God's table,
and God will rest in you.

CHARGE

The blessing and charge may be led from the doors of the church.

Walk before the Lord in faithfulness.
Follow the way of Jesus Christ.
Amen. *or* **Thanks be to God.**

Proper 16

Sunday, August 21–27

COMPLEMENTARY READINGS

Joshua 24:1–2a, 14–18   Ephesians 6:10–20
Psalm 34:15–22   John 6:56–69

OPENING SENTENCES

The eyes of the Lord are on the righteous;
God's ears are open to those who cry.
**When the righteous cry for help,
the Lord rescues them from trouble.**

The Lord is near to the brokenhearted
and saves those who are crushed in spirit.
**Many are the afflictions of the righteous,
but the Lord rescues them all.**

PRAYER OF THE DAY

Lord Jesus Christ,
by your Word and Spirit
you give life to the world.
Teach us to follow you
through every trial and trouble,
that we may believe in you
and praise your name forever. **Amen.**

INVITATION TO DISCIPLESHIP

The invitation to discipleship may be led from the baptismal font.

Joshua said to the people,
"Choose this day whom you will serve . . .
as for me and my household,
we will serve the Lord."

Friends, you are invited
to be a part of this household of faith
as we seek to love and serve the Lord.
Will you join us in the life of discipleship?

PRAYERS OF INTERCESSION

The prayers of intercession may be led from the midst of the congregation.

Holy One, you call us to be strong
in the struggle for what is right,
to stand firm in the face of evil.
Equip us with the whole armor
of the body of Christ our Lord.
God of grace, **hear our prayer.**

Give us the belt of truth,
that we may stand ready to serve you.
God of grace, **hear our prayer.**

Give us the breastplate of righteousness,
that we may be covered by your grace.
God of grace, **hear our prayer.**

Give us the shoes of a prophet,
that we may proclaim your gospel of peace.
God of grace, **hear our prayer.**

Give us the shield of faith,
that we may guard those who are vulnerable.
God of grace, **hear our prayer.**

Give us the helmet of salvation,
that we may preserve the mind of Christ.
God of grace, **hear our prayer.**

Give us the sword of the Spirit,
that we may divide truth from falsehood.
God of grace, **hear our prayer.**

By your Spirit
keep us faithful in our prayers.
By your Word
keep us faithful in our witness.
Holy God,
keep us faithful in your service.
This we pray in Jesus' name. **Amen.**

INVITATION TO OFFERING

The invitation to offering may be led from the Communion table.

It is the Spirit who gives life—
bread for all who hunger,
drink for all who thirst.

Filled with the Spirit of life,
let us offer our gifts to the Lord.

INVITATION TO THE TABLE

The invitation to the table is led from the Communion table.

Jesus said, "This is the bread
that came down from heaven.
The one who eats this bread will live forever."

People of God, come—
taste and see that the Lord is good.

CHARGE

The blessing and charge may be led from the doors of the church.

Pray in the Spirit at all times.
Share with all who are in need.
Be bold in proclaiming the gospel.
Amen. *or* **Thanks be to God.**

Proper 17

Sunday, August 28—September 3

SEMICONTINUOUS READINGS

Song of Solomon 2:8–13   James 1:17–27
Psalm 45:1–2, 6–9   Mark 7:1–8, 14–15, 21–23

OPENING SENTENCES

My heart overflows with melody!
Words of praise spring from my lips!

The throne of God endures forever.
God's rule is equity and justice.

Love righteousness and turn from evil.
God will anoint you with gladness.

PRAYER OF THE DAY

Holy One,
you call us to worship you
in spirit and in truth,
not only honoring you with our lips
but loving you in our hearts
and serving you all our lives.
Fill us with your grace,
that we may overflow with mercy
and help to heal your world;
through Jesus Christ our Lord. **Amen.**

INVITATION TO DISCIPLESHIP

The invitation to discipleship may be led from the baptismal font.

The voice of the beloved calls—
Jesus invites us to arise and follow him.

Beloved people of God, arise!
How will we answer Christ's call?

PRAYERS OF INTERCESSION

The prayers of intercession may be led from the midst of the congregation.

Generous God,
you have given birth to us
through your word of truth,
that we might bear good fruit.
Hear our prayer.

Teach us to be quick to listen,
slow to speak, and slow to anger.

Remove our wickedness from us,
and plant your word in our hearts.

Help us to be more truthful
about ourselves and your world.

Empower us to live out our faith
in ways that empower others.

Lead us in works of mercy
for those who are in distress.

All this we pray in the name of Jesus,
your Word made flesh. **Amen.**

INVITATION TO OFFERING

The invitation to offering may be led from the Communion table.

In Scripture we are called
to be doers of the word,
not merely hearers.
For if we are hearers only,
then we deceive ourselves
about who we truly are.
But if we are doers,
who act according to our faith,
we are blessed in our doing.

Therefore, let us put our faith into action.
Let us offer our lives to the Lord.

INVITATION TO THE TABLE

The invitation to the table is led from the Communion table.

The winter is past, the rain is gone.
The flowers appear on the earth,
and the turtledove is singing in the land.
The fig tree puts forth its fruit,
and the fragrant vines are in blossom.

Listen! The beloved Savior calls us.
Arise and come to the table.

CHARGE

The blessing and charge may be led from the doors of the church.

Listen for the voice of the beloved.
Let us arise and follow Jesus!
Amen. *or* **Thanks be to God.**

Proper 17

COMPLEMENTARY READINGS

Deuteronomy 4:1–2, 6–9   James 1:17–27
Psalm 15   Mark 7:1–8, 14–15, 21–23

OPENING SENTENCES

> O Lord, who may abide in your tent?
> **Who may dwell on your holy hill?**
>
> Those who walk blamelessly and do what is right;
> **those who speak the truth from their heart**
> **and do not slander with their tongues.**
>
> Those who do no evil to their neighbors;
> **those who despise wickedness but honor the Lord;**
> **those who stand by their oath at all costs.**
>
> Those who do not lend money at interest
> and do not take a bribe against the innocent.
> **Those who do these things shall never be moved.**

PRAYER OF THE DAY

> Lord Jesus Christ,
> you call us to examine our hearts
> in the light of God's law.
> Cleanse us from the inside out,
> that we may follow you faithfully
> and bear witness to your saving grace;
> in your holy name we pray. **Amen.**

INVITATION TO DISCIPLESHIP

The invitation to discipleship may be led from the baptismal font.

> God has shown us the path of life.
> We are called to follow God's way,
> to teach it to our children
> and proclaim it to all the world.
>
> You are invited to join us in this calling.
> You are invited to accompany us in this journey.
> Come and follow God with us.

PRAYERS OF INTERCESSION

The prayers of intercession may be led from the midst of the congregation.

> Living God,
> as your people in this place
> we open our hearts before you.
> God of grace, **hear our prayer.**
>
> We pray for the earth . . .
> Restore the peace of your creation.
> God of grace, **hear our prayer.**
>
> We pray for nations and leaders . . .
> Protect all who are in need.
> God of grace, **hear our prayer.**
>
> We pray for your church . . .
> Help us to proclaim the gospel.
> God of grace, **hear our prayer.**
>
> We pray for our communities . . .
> Bring peace and safety to our streets.
> God of grace, **hear our prayer.**
>
> We pray for friends and loved ones . . .
> Heal those who are sick and suffering.
> God of grace, **hear our prayer.**
>
> Living God, by your Holy Spirit
> let your Word take root within us
> and grow into a harvest of righteousness;
> through Jesus Christ our Lord. **Amen.**

INVITATION TO OFFERING

The invitation to offering may be led from the Communion table.

Every generous act of giving is from God,
and every perfect gift is from above.

People of God,
let us share the gifts of our lives
with God, the giver of life.

INVITATION TO THE TABLE

The invitation to the table is led from the Communion table.

Come to the table of the Lord.
Whether your hands are clean or dirty,
whether your heart is joyful or troubled,
whether your life is simple or complicated,
you are welcome in this place.

Jesus calls you to share this feast.
Come to the table of the Lord.

CHARGE

The blessing and charge may be led from the doors of the church.

Go and be doers of the word,
agents of God's work in the world.
This is the calling of the gospel.
Amen. *or* **Thanks be to God.**

Proper 18

Sunday, September 4–10

SEMICONTINUOUS READINGS

Proverbs 22:1–2, 8–9, 22–23   James 2:1–10 (11–13), 14–17
Psalm 125   Mark 7:24–37

OPENING SENTENCES

Those who trust in the Lord
are like Mount Zion—
a mountain that cannot be moved,
a mountain that abides forever.

As the mountains surround Jerusalem,
the Lord surrounds the people,
from this time on and forevermore.

PRAYER OF THE DAY

Gracious God,
you have opened your house
to all the nations of the world,
and you have opened your hands
to fill us with healing and grace.
Help us to open our hearts and minds
to the new thing you are doing,
that we may be ready to welcome
all people into your holy realm;
through Jesus Christ our Lord. **Amen.**

You do well if you really fulfill the royal law
according to the scripture, "You shall love your
neighbor as yourself."

James 2:8

INVITATION TO DISCIPLESHIP

The invitation to discipleship may be led from the baptismal font.

There is no favoritism, no privilege,
no partiality in the kingdom of God.
God chooses the poor to be rich in faith.
God fills the hungry with good things.
And God calls us to do the same,
loving our neighbors as ourselves.

We invite you to join this community
as we seek to live out our faith
through works of service and love.

PRAYERS OF INTERCESSION

The prayers of intercession may be led from the midst of the congregation.

God of all justice and mercy,
we seek your healing and grace,
your love to open our hearts,
your power to transform the world.
Hear our prayer.

We pray for an end to poverty . . .
Undo systems of oppression,
turn greed into generosity,
and provide abundance for all.

We pray for the restoration of the earth . . .
Teach us to be good stewards
of the earth, the water, and the air,
that all creatures may have a healthy home.

We pray for peace among neighbors . . .
Help us to repent of evil,
repair the harms we have done,
and be reconciled with one another.

We pray for loved ones . . .
Heal those who are sick,
help those who are suffering,
comfort those who mourn.

God of all justice and mercy,
give us the courage and strength
to live according to our faith
and share in your saving work;
through Jesus Christ our Lord. **Amen.**

INVITATION TO OFFERING

The invitation to offering may be led from the Communion table.

Remember the word of the Lord.
A good name is better than riches,
and favor is better than silver or gold.
The rich and the poor have this in common:
the Lord is the maker of them all.
Those who are generous are blessed,
for they share their bread with the poor.

Let us share the blessings we have received,
offering our lives to the Lord our God.

INVITATION TO THE TABLE

The invitation to the table is led from the Communion table.

A Gentile woman came to Jesus
seeking healing for her daughter.
Jesus started to turn her away, saying,
"Let the children be fed first."
But with great faith, she spoke,
"Sir, even the dogs under the table
eat the children's crumbs."
Jesus praised the woman,
and he healed her daughter.

You are invited to come to this table—
whether you come from near or far away,
whether you are filled with courage or fear,
whether you have great faith or little faith.
There are no crumbs at this table.
There is an abundant feast for everyone,
for we are all children of the living God.

CHARGE

The blessing and charge may be led from the doors of the church.

Go and tell the good news,
celebrating all that God has done.
Amen. *or* **Thanks be to God.**

Proper 18

Sunday, September 4–10

COMPLEMENTARY READINGS

Isaiah 35:4–7a   James 2:1–10 (11–13), 14–17
Psalm 146   Mark 7:24–37

OPENING SENTENCES

Praise the Lord!
Praise the Lord, O my soul!

I will praise the Lord
as long as I live;
**I will sing praises to my God
my whole life long.**

The Lord will reign forever,
**your God, O Zion,
for all generations.**

Praise the Lord!
Praise the Lord!

PRAYER OF THE DAY

Lord Jesus Christ,
you extend your mercy
to all who are in need.
Feed us at your table
and heal us by your touch,
that we may have new life
and sing your praise to all. **Amen.**

INVITATION TO DISCIPLESHIP

The invitation to discipleship may be led from the baptismal font.

The Lord our God says,
"Be strong, do not fear!
God will come and save you."

Jesus invites you
to open your eyes and ears,
to dance and sing for joy,
to come to the water of life.

PRAYERS OF INTERCESSION

The prayers of intercession may be led from the midst of the congregation.

Holy One,
we lift our hearts to you in faith,
trusting in your saving love.
God of grace, **hear our prayer.**

We pray for those who are strangers . . .
Welcome them into your holy realm.
God of grace, **hear our prayer.**

We pray for those who are poor . . .
Give them a place of honor among us.
God of grace, **hear our prayer.**

We pray for those who are naked . . .
Cover them with your goodness and grace.
God of grace, **hear our prayer.**

We pray for those who are hungry . . .
Fill them with abundant life.
God of grace, **hear our prayer.**

We pray for those who are sick . . .
Heal them with your touch.
God of grace, **hear our prayer.**

We pray for those who are in prison . . .
Visit them with compassion.
God of grace, **hear our prayer.**

Holy One,
transform these prayers into action.
Let our faith bear good fruit
in works of service and love;
through Jesus Christ our Lord. **Amen.**

INVITATION TO OFFERING

The invitation to offering may be led from the Communion table.

The Lord sets the prisoners free;
God opens the eyes of the blind.
The Lord lifts up the lowly;
God loves the righteous.
The Lord watches over the stranger;
God upholds the orphan and the widow.

Let us join the saving work of the Lord,
offering our lives and gifts to God.

INVITATION TO THE TABLE

The invitation to the table is led from the Communion table.

The Lord gives justice to the oppressed;
God provides food for those who are hungry.
Jesus turns the tables on the powers of this world,
doing what is right and helping those in need.

You are invited to share this feast—
to join this movement of justice and compassion
and then to go and share the grace of God with all.

CHARGE

The blessing and charge may be led from the doors of the church.

Let us go forth from this place
to fulfill the commandment of God:
"You shall love your neighbor as yourself."
Amen. *or* **Thanks be to God.**

Proper 19

Sunday, September 11–17

SEMICONTINUOUS READINGS

Proverbs 1:20–33   James 3:1–12
Psalm 19 *or*   Mark 8:27–38
  Wisdom 7:26–8:1

OPENING SENTENCES

> Wisdom cries out in the street;
> in the squares she raises her voice.
> **At the busiest corner she cries out;**
> **at the entrance of the city gates she speaks:**
>
> "How long, O simple ones,
> will you love being simple?
> **How long will scoffers delight in their scoffing**
> **and fools hate knowledge?**
>
> "Give heed to my reproof;
> **I will pour out my thoughts to you;**
> **I will make my words known to you."**

PRAYER OF THE DAY

> Your wisdom cries out for our attention, O Lord.
> But we look for her in all the wrong places,
> and we ignore her when she's right before our eyes.
> Make your wisdom known to us this day.
> Center us in your Word and in your Spirit,
> that we may worship you in joy and hope this day. **Amen.**

The law of the LORD is perfect, reviving the soul; the decrees of the LORD are sure, making wise the simple.

Psalm 19:7

INVITATION TO DISCIPLESHIP

The invitation to discipleship may be led from the baptismal font.

The voice of wisdom calls to us:
Come and follow me,
come and learn from me,
come and seek the ways of God.

How will you answer the call of wisdom?
How will you seek to follow the way of Jesus?
We invite you to join us on this path of discipleship.

PRAYERS OF INTERCESSION

The prayers of intercession may be led from the midst of the congregation.

The heavens tell of your glory, O God,
and the firmament proclaims your handiwork.
The days speak of your goodness,
and the nights declare knowledge of your greatness.

We join our voices with the heavens
to give you praise and thanksgiving this day.
Glory, honor, and praise be to you
for the gift of this day
and for the goodness of holy community.

Your law, O Lord, is perfect, reviving the soul.
Your decrees, O Lord, are sure, making wise the simple.
Our laws, however, are imperfect
in both their execution and their enforcement.
We seek your courage and guidance
so our laws may more correctly resemble yours,
giving justice for all, repairing wrongs of the past,
and establishing justice for the future.

Hear our prayers this day
for those burdened with anxiety, worries, illness, or grief.
Bring your healing, and restore what can be mended.
May your presence be felt in tangible ways,
and may we be your voice of love and wisdom
in the lives of those who struggle.

We join our voices with the heavens
in prayer for this world we call home
and for the places across her surface
where war, famine, disaster, and tragedy bring harm.
Help us to respond with your wisdom,
and keep us in the work even when the need feels too great.
While we cannot fix everything,
we can work to repair what is before us.
Give us courage to pay attention.

We join our voices with the heavens, O God.
Glory, honor, and praise to you. **Amen.**

INVITATION TO OFFERING

The invitation to offering may be led from the Communion table.

Let us give out of our abundance
with grateful hearts this day,
trusting that God's wisdom will use our gifts
in ways we cannot yet imagine.

INVITATION TO THE TABLE

The invitation to the table is led from the Communion table.

Jesus asked his followers,
"Who do people say that I am?"
At this table Jesus shows us who he is.
And each time we are fed
we come to understand him a little better.

You are invited to come to this table
and catch a glimpse of Jesus as Messiah—
saving us through an act of radical love.

CHARGE

The blessing and charge may be led from the doors of the church.

Go into the world on the lookout for God's wisdom
in unexpected places and from unexpected voices.
Go with courage to follow Jesus
and see where he may lead your journey.
Amen. *or* **Thanks be to God.**

Proper 19

Sunday, September 11–17

COMPLEMENTARY READINGS

Isaiah 50:4–9a   James 3:1–12
Psalm 116:1–9   Mark 8:27–38

OPENING SENTENCES

I love the Lord,
because God has heard my voice
and my supplications.
Because God inclined their ear to me,
therefore I will call on the Lord as long as I live.

Gracious is the Lord, and righteous;
our God is merciful.

Return, O my soul, to your rest,
for the Lord has dealt bountifully with you.
For God has delivered my soul from death,
my eyes from tears, my feet from stumbling.
I walk before the Lord in the land of the living.

PRAYER OF THE DAY

Incline your ear to us, O Lord.
Your grace has saved us.
As we pray, as we sing, as we worship,
may you hear the call of our hearts
reaching out toward you with gratitude. **Amen.**

Jesus went on with his disciples to the villages of
Caesarea Philippi; and on the way he asked his
disciples, "Who do people say that I am?"
Mark 8:27

INVITATION TO DISCIPLESHIP

The invitation to discipleship may be led from the baptismal font.

Jesus called the crowd with his disciples
and said to them,
"If any want to become my followers,
let them deny themselves
and take up their cross and follow me."
Today, again, Jesus invites us to become his followers.
He doesn't promise the path will be easy.
But it is a faithful path.
And there are companions on the way,
seeking to be faithful to Jesus' call.

If you're looking for a community of faith
seeking to follow Jesus,
there is room for you here.

PRAYERS OF INTERCESSION

The prayers of intercession may be led from the midst of the congregation.

Incline your ear to us, O God.
Hear us as we voice our hopes, our fears,
our fervent dreams before you now.

We offer our prayers this day
for the planet you have entrusted to our care.
Forgive us for our lazy stewardship of your creation.
Call us to care for our earth as you care for us.
Help us change our destructive ways,
that we may preserve your gift of creation.

We offer our prayers this day
for people who see the world differently than we do.
You ask us to live our lives of faith
as people who wrestle with the questions:
Who are you? What do we say about Jesus?
How are we called to live as servants together?
May we give each other grace
when we answer the questions differently.
May we trust that if we are honestly seeking you,
we will find you.

Give us humble hearts as we follow your call.
Forgive us when we bless you with our tongues
and then, with those same tongues,
curse others who are made in your image.

We offer our prayers this day
for people we know to be in need of healing,
of wholeness, of peace, of comfort, or of rest.
Help us care for each other as you care for us,
and to be agents of your grace, consolation, and hope
in the broken and wounded places of our world.

Give us hearts big enough to welcome you,
spirits trusting enough to seek you,
and minds open enough to recognize you
when you draw near to us. **Amen.**

INVITATION TO OFFERING

The invitation to offering may be led from the Communion table.

When asked, "Who do we say Jesus is?"
people will have different answers.
And that's okay.
One thing we know here
is that when we offer our time in service,
our hearts in worship,
and our minds in study and prayer,
we get closer to understanding Jesus.
We get closer to God when we get closer to each other.

As our offering is received this morning,
know that our pledges, tithes, and offerings
help us sense God more clearly
as they enable us to grow our community,
our witness, and our outreach.
Let us give with generous hearts
as we seek to know Jesus better, together.

INVITATION TO THE TABLE

The invitation to the table is led from the Communion table.

Jesus keeps showing us the way of peace,
but we keep trusting the way of war.
Jesus keeps telling us there is enough for all,
but we keep living in selfishness and fear.

At this table there is grace and peace.
At this table there is plenty for all.
Through this life-giving meal,
we follow Jesus into a world of abundance and hope.
Come, be fed.

CHARGE

The blessing and charge may be led from the doors of the church.

Gracious is the Lord, and righteous;
our God is merciful.
The Lord protects the simple;
when we are brought low, God saves us.
Return your soul to God,
for the Lord has dealt bountifully with you.
The Lord has delivered our souls from death,
our eyes from tears, our feet from stumbling.
Call on the Lord as long as you live.
Go in peace and walk before the Lord
in the land of the living.
Amen. *or* **Thanks be to God.**

Proper 20

Sunday, September 18–24

SEMICONTINUOUS READINGS

Proverbs 31:10–31	James 3:13–4:3, 7–8a
Psalm 1	Mark 9:30–37

OPENING SENTENCES

Who is wise and understanding among you?
Show by your good life
that your works are done
with gentleness born of wisdom.
Wisdom from above is first pure,
then peaceable, gentle, willing to yield,
full of mercy and good fruits,
without a trace of partiality or hypocrisy.

And a harvest of righteousness is sown in peace
for those who make peace.
Draw near to God,
and God will draw near to you.

PRAYER OF THE DAY

Holy Wisdom, we seek you.
Too often we take shortcuts
and seek the easy route,
the path of less conflict,
the road to fame and glory.
This day, center us in your wisdom,
that we may worship you in joy and humility,
turning our hearts to the servant's path. **Amen.**

INVITATION TO DISCIPLESHIP

The invitation to discipleship may be led from the baptismal font.

Happy are those who seek wisdom,
delighting in the law of the Lord.
Happy are those who take root and grow
beside streams of living water.

The goodness, truth, and beauty of God
are for all people.
Come and seek God's way of wisdom
with this community of faith.

PRAYERS OF INTERCESSION

The prayers of intercession may be led from the midst of the congregation.

Holy Wisdom,
we spend too much time and energy
worrying about things
that are largely outside of our control.
We spend too little time trusting you, O God,
and too little time living the life you call us to lead.
We get turned around and things seem muddled.

Help us to trust in you rather than our own wisdom,
so we may have abundance in our lives,
making room for the well-being of people
beyond our own circles.

Hear our prayers for the world
in which we live, love, struggle, triumph, and suffer.
We know that you are in all things,
so help us to sense you
when we feel alone in our pain.
Help us to sense you
when we feel alone in our accomplishments too.
Help us to sense you
in the suffering of our neighbors,
that we may reach out to help.
Help us to sense you
in the injustices of our society,
that we may work for change.

Help us to recognize your wisdom
in the people we least expect to have it—
even from the people we most want to judge.
Help us to see your divine image
in the people the world calls foolish,
knowing that you love all of your children.
We have never met someone you do not love.
We will never meet someone you do not love.

Humbly, we pray. **Amen.**

INVITATION TO OFFERING

The invitation to offering may be led from the Communion table.

The psalmist says we are happy
when we do not follow the advice of the wicked
or take the path that sinners tread.
We're called to delight in the law of the Lord,
and to meditate on God's law day and night.
When we do, the psalmist says,
we will be like trees planted by streams of water,
yielding good fruit in due season.
In all that we do, we will prosper.

As our offering is received this morning,
know that our pledges, tithes, and offerings
contribute to the harvest.
A harvest of righteousness is sown in peace
for those who make peace.
Let us give with joyful hearts,
happy to contribute to a harvest
that is bigger than any of us could do on our own.

INVITATION TO THE TABLE

The invitation to the table is led from the Communion table.

As Jesus and his disciples wandered through the towns,
healing and casting out demons,
they also discussed difficult topics,
such as his impending betrayal and death.
We shouldn't underestimate the challenges
of being one of his disciples.
He also picked up a little child,
and taking it in his arms he said to them,
"Whoever welcomes one such child in my name
welcomes me,
and whoever welcomes me
welcomes not me but the one who sent me."

Alongside the challenges of discipleship,
God also embraces us as a parent holds a child,
welcoming us in an embrace
of unconditional love and grace.
At this table we are like children
called home after a full day at school
and an afternoon of riding bikes with friends,
to find that a meal has been prepared for us.
All we have to do is wash our hands and come to the table.

Whatever the stresses and worries
and joys and excitement of our lives,
here we gather as God's children
for the meal prepared for us.
As we come to the table today,
let us do so as children welcomed home by God.
And as we leave the table today,
let us do so with an intention
to welcome others as God's children too.
As we are fed, let us feed the world
in joy and hope.

CHARGE

The blessing and charge may be led from the doors of the church.

Go into the world as children
who have been welcomed home by God.
Extend that welcome to a hurting world.
Trust the wisdom of God
and the goodness of God
and the grace of God.
It is sufficient for us.
Amen. *or* **Thanks be to God.**

Proper 20

Sunday, September 18–24

COMPLEMENTARY READINGS

Wisdom 1:16–2:1, 12–22 *or*   James 3:13–4:3, 7–8a
  Jeremiah 11:18–20   Mark 9:30–37
Psalm 54

OPENING SENTENCES

Who is wise and understanding among you?
Show by your good life
that your works are done
with gentleness born of wisdom.

Wisdom from above is first pure,
then peaceable, gentle, willing to yield,
full of mercy and good fruits,
without a trace of partiality or hypocrisy.
And a harvest of righteousness
is sown in peace
for those who make peace.

Draw near to God,
and God will draw near to you.

PRAYER OF THE DAY

Holy Wisdom, we seek you.
Too often we take shortcuts
and seek the easy route,
the path of less conflict,
the road to fame and glory.
This day, center us in your truth,
that we may worship you with joy and humility,
turning our hearts to the servant's path. **Amen.**

INVITATION TO DISCIPLESHIP

The invitation to discipleship may be led from the baptismal font.

Some days we don't understand
what Jesus is saying to us,
and we are afraid to ask.
That is when it is helpful
to have the gift of a faith community.
It can be a place where
we can bring our honest questions,
our doubts, our worries, and our hopes—
and where we can find support,
understanding, and other people
who are also figuring things out.

Come and join us.
We haven't figured everything out,
but we are seeking to do so together.
There is room for you here.

PRAYERS OF INTERCESSION

The prayers of intercession may be led from the midst of the congregation.

Save us, O God, by your name,
and vindicate us by your might.
Hear our prayers, O God;
give ear to the words of our mouths.
You are the upholder of our lives,
and so we offer ourselves to you.

We seek your wisdom, O God.
Take away the bitter envy
and selfish ambition in our hearts,
and fill us with gentleness born of wisdom.
Your wisdom is first pure,
then peaceable, gentle, willing to yield,
full of mercy and good fruits,
without a trace of partiality or hypocrisy.

We cry out for a justice that leads to peace.
Help us remember that
a harvest of righteousness is sown in peace
for those who make peace.
Send us into your world,
that we may be your agents of peace
to people in pain, people in conflict,
and people grieving injustices that lead to harm.
Your peace is greater than we can imagine,
and we are bold enough to call for it.
Bring your peace into warring hearts and nations,
into broken hearts and communities,
into grieving hearts and families.

Hear our prayers this day
for those we know to be in need of your peace,
for those who have shown us your wisdom,
and for those who seek healing.

We would draw near to you, O God.
Please draw near to us. **Amen.**

INVITATION TO OFFERING

The invitation to offering may be led from the Communion table.

As our offering is received this morning,
let us give with generous hearts,
offering back to God a portion of our harvest.

INVITATION TO THE TABLE

The invitation to the table is led from the Communion table.

Scripture tells us, "Draw near to God,
and God will draw near to you."
God draws near to us in myriad ways,
including the kindness of friend or stranger,
the stillness of prayer,
the joyful embrace of loved ones,
and the feast of God's table.
Here we are fed, we are nourished,
and we celebrate the gift of God's abundant love—
poured out for us in the living, the dying,
and the resurrection of Jesus.

Let us draw near to the God
who has drawn near to us.
Come and be fed.

CHARGE

The blessing and charge may be led from the doors of the church.

Who is wise and understanding among you?
Show by your good life
that your works are done with gentleness
born of wisdom.

When we seek God's wisdom,
a harvest of righteousness will be sown in peace
for those who make peace.

So go in peace,
working for a harvest of righteousness.
Go in wisdom,
seeking hearts that are gentle and humble.
Draw near to God,
and God will draw near to you.
Amen. *or* **Thanks be to God.**

Proper 21

Sunday, September 25—October 1

SEMICONTINUOUS READINGS

Esther 7:1–6, 9–10; 9:20–22   James 5:13–20
Psalm 124   Mark 9:38–50

OPENING SENTENCES

Today Jesus invites us
to join with our siblings in faith
in a deeper faithfulness—
**to pursue a life of perseverance
in the face of challenge,
of generosity in circumstances of scarcity,
of steadfastness in the midst of uncertainty.**

Let us receive this invitation
as a sign of the trust that God has in us,
to grow, to learn, to serve, and to be transformed.
Let us worship God.

PRAYER OF THE DAY

Faithful God,
when it seems that the walls are closing in,
the resources are drying up,
and failure is certain,
help us to steady one another in our faith.
Let us not be distracted
by those circumstances or people
that would lead us to be fear-driven
in our perspective.
Rather, in the face of these,
empower us to be generous,
gracious, and open-hearted,
so that we might all the more
reflect your goodness. **Amen.**

INVITATION TO DISCIPLESHIP

The invitation to discipleship may be led from the baptismal font.

> Discipleship is a journey
> of perseverance and possibility.
> It is how we grow deeper in faith and faithfulness.
>
> If you desire to be deeply rooted in God's love
> so that you can be more broadly used
> for God's life-giving purpose,
> receive Christ's invitation to follow him today.

PRAYERS OF INTERCESSION

The prayers of intercession may be led from the midst of the congregation.

> Loving God, we lift up to you this day
> the ways in which we struggle to trust your goodness.
> Our world is filled with wars and rumors of war,
> pain and the perpetuation of pain,
> fear and the commodification of fear.
> Help us, in the haze of all that would cloud our imaginations,
> to maintain our gaze on your call
> not only to survive but to participate
> in building a world where all can thrive.
> So hear us now
> as we lift up to you those circumstances and situations
> that trouble our hearts and hold us back.
>
> For our governments and leaders . . .
> We ask, O God, that you would convict them
> of the heavy mantle which lies upon their shoulders,
> that they might understand their work
> as essential practices for helping to shape a world
> where all can thrive.
> Help us to hold them accountable
> to this sacred call of civic caretaking,
> and empower us to participate in that work.

For our community leaders . . .
Empower, encourage, and equip those in our midst who—
through formal and informal status—
help to forge connections of relationship,
culture-building, and mutuality among us.
Through their leadership and love,
we ask that the threads which weave our social fabric
might be reknit and reinforced.

For one another . . .
Help us to see one another better,
making space for that which we may not fully understand
but deeply need to know.
Open our hearts to receive ourselves and one another
with greater compassion, curiosity, and grace,
that in our spiritual hospitality
we might encounter you anew.

In your holy name we pray. **Amen.**

INVITATION TO OFFERING

The invitation to offering may be led from the Communion table.

Jesus proclaims that
no matter where we are in our journey,
we can participate in God's good work
of caring for one another's well-being,
that what we have is not only for ourselves
but for the nourishment of all.

At this time you are invited
to participate in that work
through the offering of your gifts—
for the sake of this gathered community
and the communities in which we live.

INVITATION TO THE TABLE

The invitation to the table is led from the Communion table.

Jesus instructed his disciples
to never lose their saltiness,
that in so doing
they might find greater peace with one another.
Salt preserves,
helps us to maintain hydration,
and enhances flavor.
All of these are ways of maintaining
the goodness, integrity, and well-being
of that which we partake.

At this table we enjoy the gifts
of those who came before—
preserving, enhancing, and maintaining
the integrity of the faith that we proclaim.

CHARGE

The blessing and charge may be led from the doors of the church.

Go forward from this place
empowered and encouraged,
as you work alongside others
who seek God's goodwill in the world.
Do not be discouraged or lose your flavor,
but recall the one who labors alongside you
for the sake of a world that hungers for the bread of life.
Amen. *or* **Thanks be to God.**

Proper 21

Sunday, September 25—October 1

COMPLEMENTARY READINGS

Numbers 11:4–6, 10–16, 24–29
Psalm 19:7–14

James 5:13–20
Mark 9:38–50

OPENING SENTENCES

The law of the Lord is perfect;
the decrees of the Lord are sure.

The precepts of the Lord are right;
the commandment of the Lord is clear.

The fear of the Lord is pure;
the ordinances of the Lord are true.

Let us worship the Lord,
who revives the soul
and makes wise the simple,
who rejoices the heart
and enlightens the eyes,
who endures forever
and is righteous altogether.
Let us worship God.

PRAYER OF THE DAY

O Lord our God, we give you thanks
that you have poured out your Spirit
upon all people, giving us power
to speak the truth and do what is right.
Deliver us from all sin and evil,
and lead us in paths of righteousness,
that we may be faithful followers
of Jesus Christ our Savior. **Amen.**

INVITATION TO DISCIPLESHIP

The invitation to discipleship may be led from the baptismal font.

Jesus welcomed all who shared the vision
of God's realm of grace and peace.
Indeed, Jesus taught his disciples,
"Whoever is not against us is for us."

Do you share the vision? We welcome you.
Join us as we seek to follow Christ.

PRAYERS OF INTERCESSION

The prayers of intercession may be led from the midst of the congregation.

Remembering the words of James,
we bring our whole lives to God in prayer,
saying: Lord of life, **hear our prayer.**

We pray for those who are suffering . . .
Give strength to those who are weak
and justice to all who are oppressed.
Lord of life, **hear our prayer.**

We rejoice with those who are cheerful . . .
Continue to bless them with peace,
and fill their hearts with songs of praise.
Lord of life, **hear our prayer.**

We ask healing for those who are sick . . .
Show mercy to those who are ill,
and raise them up to health and life.
Lord of life, **hear our prayer.**

We seek forgiveness from our sin . . .
Teach us to turn away from evil
and turn toward your holy way.
Lord of life, **hear our prayer.**

We pray for this wounded earth . . .
Pour out your life-giving grace
that all creation may be restored.
Lord of life, **hear our prayer.**

For the gift of prayer, O God, we give you thanks.
Receive all the prayers of your people,
that they may be powerful and effective;
through the righteousness of Jesus Christ. **Amen.**

INVITATION TO OFFERING

The invitation to offering may be led from the Communion table.

Jesus said:
"Whoever gives you a cup of water to drink
because you bear the name of Christ
will by no means lose the reward."

As disciples of Christ Jesus,
let us share the grace of God with all
through the offering of our lives and gifts.

INVITATION TO THE TABLE

The invitation to the table is led from the Communion table.

In the wilderness God sustained us
with daily bread, manna from heaven.
At this table God nourishes us
with the bread of life, Jesus Christ.

Come, taste and see
the goodness and grace of God.

CHARGE

The blessing and charge may be led from the doors of the church.

Let the words of your mouth,
the thoughts of your heart,
and the works of your hands
be acceptable to the Lord,
our rock and our redeemer.
Amen. *or* **Thanks be to God.**

Proper 22

Sunday, October 2–8

SEMICONTINUOUS READINGS

Job 1:1; 2:1–10   Hebrews 1:1–4; 2:5–12
Psalm 26   Mark 10:2–16

OPENING SENTENCES

> Our God is a God of hospitality—
> inviting, welcoming, and embracing all
> who seek to know her better.
> **There is no prerequisite, qualification,
> or application required for the encounter;
> you just have to want to come.**
>
> So come and experience the radical grace
> of belonging in Jesus Christ.
> **We come to worship God.**

PRAYER OF THE DAY

> God who sees us, help us to see you.
> When we feel distanced from one another
> and from ourselves, meet us—
> stir up within us an awareness of your presence
> that cuts through our isolation.
> Meet us there and meet us here,
> that we might know there is no place we can go
> that is too far from Love's reach. **Amen.**

> *There was once a man in the land of Uz whose
> name was Job. That man was blameless and upright,
> one who feared God and turned away from evil.*
>
> *Job 1:1*

INVITATION TO DISCIPLESHIP

The invitation to discipleship may be led from the baptismal font.

God invites us to a faithfulness
that abides through even the most challenging seasons of life.
And yet it is in such times
when we can come to know
God's enduring grace and anchoring peace,
surpassing all understanding.

If you desire to know this kind of grace,
if you seek such peace,
receive God's invitation to faithfulness
and let it transform your inner being for outer purpose.

PRAYERS OF INTERCESSION

The prayers of intercession may be led from the midst of the congregation.

Faithful God, we confess that
at times your ways can feel confusing.
We need not look long at the world and our communities
in order to see the ways in which you feel absent.
We join the psalmist in claiming your faithful love
and ask that you would move on your promises of justice,
of wholeness of life for all,
of the power to overcome and persevere
through even the greatest of trials,
that in our perseverance
we might bear witness to and proclaim
your sustaining grace.
Hear our prayer.

We pray for our world . . .
that you would grant us a vision
that is greater than what we can see
in this present moment,
that we might have a prophetic imagination
to fuel our efforts.

We pray for our cities and towns . . .
that you might help us to choose engagement
with those in our communities,
knowing that as we do,
we strengthen the fabric of connection
which helps us all to thrive.

Finally, we pray for our church . . .
that you would keep us present to one another
and help us to embody your call to commitment
with a prophetic joy that identifies and amplifies
the ways in which you are acting for wholeness of life.

In all of these and so much more, O God,
we ask your generous and abundant activity
to draw your creation closer
to that which you created it to be. **Amen.**

INVITATION TO OFFERING

The invitation to offering may be led from the Communion table.

God calls us to participate
in God's work of wholeness-making
with all that we have to offer.
In this we find purpose, sacrifice, and joy.
In this we carry forward
that which our ancestors in the faith
offered on our behalf.

At this time you are invited
to share your gifts,
adding to the good work
that God invites us to share,
across generations.

INVITATION TO THE TABLE

The invitation to the table is led from the Communion table.

At this table we remember that
even as Jesus is above all things
and over all things,
even as all things hang together in Christ,
we are invited to dine with him
as friends, as partners, and as inheritors of his grace.

We gather at this table as cocreators
in God's vision of wholeness of life for all.
We gather in joy, we gather in grief,
we gather in despair, and we gather in faith,
to be nourished once again
by the bread of life and the cup of God's promise.

CHARGE

The blessing and charge may be led from the doors of the church.

Go forward from this place, knowing that the one
who is the pioneer and perfecter of our faith goes before us.
Be encouraged in this grace,
be bold in your faithfulness,
and be steadfast in your trust
that God walks with you through every season.
Amen. *or* **Thanks be to God.**

Proper 22

COMPLEMENTARY READINGS

Genesis 2:18–24   Hebrews 1:1–4; 2:5–12
Psalm 8   Mark 10:2–16

OPENING SENTENCES

> O Lord our God,
> your majesty is known in all the earth!
> **O Lord our God,**
> **your glory shines above the heavens!**
>
> What are human beings
> that you are mindful of them?
> **Who are mortals**
> **that you care for them?**
>
> Yet you have crowned them
> with glory and honor.
> **You have called them to care**
> **for the works of your hands.**

PRAYER OF THE DAY

> Loving God,
> you created us for relationship
> and call us to live as partners—
> with you, with one another,
> and with all the creatures of the earth.
> Teach us to live in love
> and share your love with others,
> that all things may be one;
> through Jesus Christ our Lord. **Amen.**

INVITATION TO DISCIPLESHIP

The invitation to discipleship may be led from the baptismal font.

Jesus said,
"Let the little children come to me;
do not stop them,
for it is to such as these
that the kingdom of God belongs."

Jesus calls you
to receive the realm of God
with childlike wonder and faith.
How will you respond to his call?

PRAYERS OF INTERCESSION

The prayers of intercession may be led from the midst of the congregation.

God of majesty and glory,
hear the prayers of your people.

We pray for the earth . . .
Guide us to protect all creatures:
the beasts of the field,
birds of the air, and fish of the sea.

We pray for the church . . .
Unite us in your worship and service,
and what you have joined together
let no one separate.

We pray for our neighbors . . .
Teach us to cherish all people
as your beloved children,
citizens of your holy realm.

We pray for our loved ones . . .
Help us to love and care for one another
in abundance and in poverty,
in sickness and in health.

Hear the prayers of your people,
God of majesty and glory;
through Jesus Christ our Lord. **Amen.**

INVITATION TO OFFERING

The invitation to offering may be led from the Communion table.

We are called to care for the earth
and to share God's grace with all.

Let us offer our lives to the Lord.

INVITATION TO THE TABLE

The invitation to the table is led from the Communion table.

This is the feast of the new creation—
where heaven and earth are united,
where justice and peace embrace,
where we become one flesh
in the body and blood of Christ.

Come to the table, children of God.
Receive the gifts of God's realm.

CHARGE

The blessing and charge may be led from the doors of the church.

Go in peace and love
to share the message of reconciliation
in Jesus Christ our Lord.
Amen. *or* **Thanks be to God.**

Proper 23

SEMICONTINUOUS READINGS

Job 23:1–9, 16–17   Hebrews 4:12–16
Psalm 22:1–15   Mark 10:17–31

OPENING SENTENCES

My God, I cry to you.
Holy One, hear my prayer.

In you our ancestors trusted;
they trusted, and you delivered them.
To you they cried and were saved;
in you they trusted
and were not put to shame.

On you I was cast from my birth,
and since my mother bore me
you have been my God.
Do not be far from me,
for trouble is near.

PRAYER OF THE DAY

Almighty God,
in days of groaning and grief,
we cry out for your help,
trusting that, with you,
all things are possible.
Show us your mercy,
strengthen our faint hearts,
and deliver us from evil,
that we may follow you faithfully;
through Christ our Lord. **Amen.**

INVITATION TO DISCIPLESHIP

The invitation to discipleship may be led from the baptismal font.

How hard is it to enter the kingdom of God?
For mortals, it is impossible, but not for God;
for God all things are possible.

Through Jesus Christ,
God has invited us into the kingdom.
Will you join us in answering the call?

PRAYERS OF INTERCESSION

The prayers of intercession may be led from the midst of the congregation.

In Jesus Christ we have a great high priest
who has passed through the heavens.
Let us join Christ's intercession for the world.

We pray for the church . . .
Keep us faithful in following Christ;
let us be a sign of your kingdom,
that all may know your saving love.

We pray for the nations . . .
Change the hearts of our leaders;
bring justice and establish equity,
that all may have abundant life.

We pray for our communities . . .
Bind up our brokenness;
put an end to all violence,
that people may live in safety.

We pray for friends and family . . .
Comfort those who are suffering;
give them healing and peace,
that they may sing your praise.

Help us, God of grace,
to seek your will and follow your way,
to bear witness to your saving work
and welcome your new creation.
All this and more we pray through Christ,
our great high priest. **Amen.**

INVITATION TO OFFERING

The invitation to offering may be led from the Communion table.

A man asked Jesus, "Good Teacher,
what must I do to inherit eternal life?"
Jesus said, "You lack one thing;
go, sell what you own,
and give the money to the poor,
and you will have treasure in heaven;
then come, follow me."

Let us respond to Christ's call
through the offering of our lives.

INVITATION TO THE TABLE

The invitation to the table is led from the Communion table.

At the table of the Lord
the first are last and the last are first.
Here we honor the wisdom of children,
treasure the gifts of the poor,
welcome people who are outcast,
and fill the hungry with good things.

Come with empty hands and open hearts.
Christ will meet you at this table.

CHARGE

The blessing and charge may be led from the doors of the church.

Let us hold fast to our faith,
trusting that all things are possible for God.
Amen. *or* **Thanks be to God.**

Proper 23

Sunday, October 9–15

COMPLEMENTARY READINGS

Amos 5:6–7, 10–15   Hebrews 4:12–16
Psalm 90:12–17   Mark 10:17–31

OPENING SENTENCES

Merciful One, we turn to you:
Turn to us, O Lord!

Satisfy us with your steadfast love,
so we may rejoice in you.

Teach us to count our days,
so we may gain wisdom and understanding.

Merciful One, we turn to you:
Turn to us, O Lord!

PRAYER OF THE DAY

Good Teacher,
we have followed your word,
we have kept your commandments,
and we come now to you—
longing to learn
and seeking the good you offer.
Mold us in this time together,
that we might better follow you. **Amen.**

*They were greatly astounded and said to one another,
"Then who can be saved?" Jesus looked at them and
said, "For mortals it is impossible, but not for God;
for God all things are possible."*

Mark 10:26–27

INVITATION TO DISCIPLESHIP

The invitation to discipleship may be led from the baptismal font.

We hear the call to let go of our possessions,
to give to those in need and follow,
and it feels daunting.
We fear losing our first-place status
and becoming last.
But the God who calls us to this life
is not far off and distant.
Christ sympathizes with us,
has been tested like us,
knows what it's like to live this life.

God invites you to this radical life
of compassion and humility.
Christ will meet you there.

PRAYERS OF INTERCESSION

The prayers of intercession may be led from the midst of the congregation.

God of justice and righteousness,
we will seek you.

When the evils of the world are impossible to face,
when the struggles of our lives are too much to carry,
when the challenges of those we love break our hearts,
God of justice and righteousness,
we will seek you.

When we feel the thrill of new life and new possibilities,
when we relax into a season of plenty,
when we celebrate and rejoice with each other,
God of justice and righteousness,
we will seek you.

When we are the ones causing others to hurt,
when we do not notice the effects of our actions,
when we turn away in self-interest,
God of justice and righteousness,
we will seek you.

Guide us in our journeys
and be gracious to us,
that we may live lives worthy of your name. **Amen.**

INVITATION TO OFFERING

The invitation to offering may be led from the Communion table.

In this time of offering,
we acknowledge and honor the ways
that God has brought prosperity into our lives.

Let us give back a portion of that prosperity,
that others may experience the grace of God.

INVITATION TO THE TABLE

The invitation to the table is led from the Communion table.

We get caught up
in trying to earn a place at this table.
We think that if we just do the right things,
say the right words,
give up what should be given up
and take on what should be taken on,
maybe one day we will be worthy of this feast.
Yes, it is important
to care and give,
and praise and pray,
and let go and trust,
but it is not our job to save ourselves,
and this table is not about worth.

For us it is impossible,
but for God all things are possible.
God has chosen to use that possibility
to spread a table for us—
where we gather just as we are
to find peace and wholeness.

CHARGE

The blessing and charge may be led from the doors of the church.

Seek good and not evil!
The God of hosts will be with us.
Amen. *or* **Thanks be to God.**

Proper 24

Sunday, October 16–22

SEMICONTINUOUS READINGS

Job 38:1–7 (34–41)   Hebrews 5:1–10

Psalm 104:1–9, 24, 35c   Mark 10:35–45

OPENING SENTENCES

Come, let us worship God,
who created all things!
We worship God,
who laid the foundations of the earth,

who makes the morning stars sing together,
who sends forth lightning,

and who gives wisdom and understanding.
Let us lift our voices in praise.

PRAYER OF THE DAY

Our souls bless you, O God—
for your imagination that created us,
your wisdom that guides us,
your example that inspires us.
Help us to follow your way,
to mold our lives after yours
and reflect your image to all we meet. **Amen.**

In the days of his flesh, Jesus offered up prayers and
supplications, with loud cries and tears, to the one
who was able to save him from death, and he was
heard because of his reverent submission.

Hebrews 5:7

INVITATION TO DISCIPLESHIP

The invitation to discipleship may be led from the baptismal font.

We worship a God who is cosmic:
stretching out the heavens, setting the stars.
We worship a God who is near us:
who lived with us, knowing our suffering.

How can you honor the God who created all things
in your practice this week?
How can you honor the God of humanity and relationship
in your practice this week?

PRAYERS OF INTERCESSION

The prayers of intercession may be led from the midst of the congregation.

Son of Man,
following you can be hard.
We expect prosperity but find poverty.
We expect a conqueror but find a sacrifice.
We expect glory but find humility.

Help us to set aside our expectations.
Help us to do the work.
Help us to be servants instead of rulers.

Help us to serve:

those who are sick and need care . . .

those who have no home and need shelter . . .

those who are lonely and need companionship . . .

those who are underpaid and need support . . .

those who are scared and need reassurance . . .

We hardly know what we are asking,
but we look to you with trust and hope
for the possibilities of what this world can be.

Help us be able to follow you. **Amen.**

INVITATION TO OFFERING

The invitation to offering may be led from the Communion table.

We do not come to this sacred space
to re-create the hierarchies of the world.
We do not come to hoard what we have
and lord it over all who have less.
We come to offer and give thanks.
We come to acknowledge the blessings we have been given
and to let them go so that they may be blessings to others.

In this spirit let us offer our gifts to God.

INVITATION TO THE TABLE

The invitation to the table is led from the Communion table.

Those who stand at this table,
offering this bread and cup,
are not the owners of this table.
The ones who keep it set in this place
are not the keepers of salvation.

That is Christ, our great high priest,
who does not glorify himself,
demanding our sacrifice and submission,
but rather sits with us—
the source of eternal salvation
reaching out to us saying,
"Come! I am so glad you are here."

CHARGE

The blessing and charge may be led from the doors of the church.

Go, not to be served but to serve.
We go with God's grace.
Amen. *or* **Thanks be to God.**

Proper 24

Sunday, October 16–22

COMPLEMENTARY READINGS

Isaiah 53:4–12	Hebrews 5:1–10
Psalm 91:9–16	Mark 10:35–45

OPENING SENTENCES

The Lord is our strength and refuge;
God's presence is with us!

When we call on the name of God,
God will answer!

God's salvation will be revealed.
Praise the Lord!

PRAYER OF THE DAY

Loving God, your promises are steadfast and sure.
As we gather for worship,
make your presence known among us.
Give us hearts to love and serve you.
Through the presence of the Holy Spirit
may we become witnesses to your grace and compassion.
We ask this in the name
of your Son and our Savior, Jesus Christ. **Amen.**

INVITATION TO DISCIPLESHIP

The invitation to discipleship may be led from the baptismal font.

Jesus says,
"Whoever wishes to become great among you
must be your servant."

Will you become a servant of God?
If you are ready and willing
to offer your God-given gifts and talents
to serve others,
we welcome you into this community of faith.

PRAYERS OF INTERCESSION

The prayers of intercession may be led from the midst of the congregation.

We serve a God who listens to us
when we lift up our intercessions
for ourselves and the world.
Let us go to God in confidence.

O God, we pray for this world
in need of your guidance . . .

O God, we pray for the neighbors we know
and those we have yet to meet . . .

O God, we pray for our elected leaders,
that they will follow your will . . .

O God, we pray for those who are suffering
from illness and pain . . .

O God, we pray for our communities of faith . . .

O God, we pray for justice
for those who are oppressed . . .

Hear our prayer, O God.
Receive these prayers, and assure us
that our intercessions will not be in vain.
Strengthen us by your grace to live in faith
this day and forevermore.
We ask this in the name
of our Lord and Savior, Jesus Christ. **Amen.**

INVITATION TO OFFERING

The invitation to offering may be led from the Communion table.

Each of you must give as you have made up your mind,
not reluctantly or under compulsion,
for God loves a cheerful giver.

Through this offering, let us return
a portion of what God has given to us.

INVITATION TO THE TABLE

The invitation to the table is led from the Communion table.

The Lord is gracious and merciful!
Before us are the gifts of God
for the people of God.
Whether you are from the north or south,
the east or west,
you are invited to sit at this table.

Our Savior invites all those who trust him
to share in this feast that he has prepared.

CHARGE

The blessing and charge may be led from the doors of the church.

Remember that you are called
not to be served, but to serve others.
Go and serve the Lord.
Amen. *or* **Thanks be to God.**

Proper 25

Sunday, October 23–29

SEMICONTINUOUS READINGS

Job 42:1–6, 10–17   Hebrews 7:23–28

Psalm 34:1–8 (19–22)   Mark 10:46–52

OPENING SENTENCES

Gathered people of God,
let us bless the Lord,
now and at all times!
O magnify the Lord with me;
let us exalt God's name forever.

May our souls boast in the Lord!
Let the humble hear and be glad.

PRAYER OF THE DAY

God who has called us here,
we long for the hope and healing
we know you offer when we cry to you.
Meet us in this time
and strengthen our faith,
that we may follow you on the way. **Amen.**

INVITATION TO DISCIPLESHIP

The invitation to discipleship may be led from the baptismal font.

We take heart because Christ has called us.
Christ has offered us new life and new opportunities,
new visions and new dreams.

Are you ready to accept that offering?
Are you ready to receive new life and follow?

PRAYERS OF INTERCESSION

The prayers of intercession may be led from the midst of the congregation.

Restore us, O God.
Restore us, O God.

This world has known loss:
the loss of species and cultures,
the loss of lands and home,
the loss of lives and relationships.
Restore us, O God.

This community has known loss:
the loss of jobs and security,
the loss of neighbors and friends,
the loss of health and hope.
Restore us, O God.

Grant this community:
the joy of coming together,
the strength of collaboration,
the triumph of resilience.
Restore us, O God.

Grant this world:
the resolve of repentance,
the beauty of reclamation,
the hope of new life.
Restore us, O God. Amen.

INVITATION TO OFFERING

The invitation to offering may be led from the Communion table.

In our lives we have sought God,
and God has answered.
God rescues us from our afflictions
and redeems our lives.

Let us offer our thanks and praise!

INVITATION TO THE TABLE

The invitation to the table is led from the Communion table.

This table is not a place of sacrifices and atonement;
God has no need for sacrifices.
Though we are imperfect, a perfect God
came for us and for our salvation.

The altar transforms into the table.
The sacrifice has become the great feast!

CHARGE

The blessing and charge may be led from the doors of the church.

Go! Your faith has made you well.
Let us follow in God's way.
Amen. *or* **Thanks be to God.**

Proper 25

Sunday, October 23–29

COMPLEMENTARY READINGS

Jeremiah 31:7–9   Hebrews 7:23–28
Psalm 126   Mark 10:46–52

OPENING SENTENCES

When the Lord restores our fortunes
we will dream again.

We will laugh and shout for joy, proclaiming,
"The Lord has done great things!"

Let us rejoice in the Lord our God,
for the Lord has done great things!

PRAYER OF THE DAY

Almighty God,
you are the one to whom we sing
with gladness and joy.
We thank you for all things, great and small,
as we gather today.
May your Holy Spirit be upon us
as we worship you in spirit and truth,
that we may become witnesses
of your love in the world.
We pray this in the name
of our Lord and Savior, Jesus Christ. **Amen.**

*May those who sow in tears reap with shouts of joy. Those
who go out weeping, bearing the seed for sowing, shall come
home with shouts of joy, carrying their sheaves.*

Psalm 126:5–6

INVITATION TO DISCIPLESHIP

The invitation to discipleship may be led from the baptismal font.

As the people said to Bartimaeus,
"Take heart; get up, he is calling you."
Jesus continually calls us
to follow and serve others.

If you feel that God is calling you
to discipleship in this community,
we welcome you.

PRAYERS OF INTERCESSION

The prayers of intercession may be led from the midst of the congregation.

In Jesus Christ we have a great high priest
who lives to make intercession for us.
Let us lift our prayers to the Lord.

We pray for the church,
the body of Christ here on earth . . .

We pray for our families,
those by blood and those by friendship . . .

We pray for the earth,
that we may be responsible stewards of creation . . .

We pray for those who are imprisoned unjustly,
that one day they may be free . . .

We pray for those who are suffering from addiction,
that they may find healing . . .

May your Holy Spirit move in us,
that we may believe that our prayers are heard.
Strengthen us to go forth in faith and serve you.
We ask this through Jesus Christ our Lord. **Amen.**

INVITATION TO OFFERING

The invitation to offering may be led from the Communion table.

The Lord has done great things for us,
and we have rejoiced!

With grateful hearts and minds,
let us return our thanks and praise to God
through the offering of our gifts.

INVITATION TO THE TABLE

The invitation to the table is led from the Communion table.

Beloved, the Lord is good
and is worthy to be praised!
You are invited to this table.
The Lord is going to gather us
from the north, south, east, and west.
The Lord will invite all people
from all walks of life
to partake of these gracious gifts.

Come and share these gifts of God
at the table Christ prepares for us.

CHARGE

The blessing and charge may be led from the doors of the church.

Rejoice in the Lord always!
Amen. *or* **Thanks be to God.**

Proper 26

Sunday, October 30—November 5

SEMICONTINUOUS READINGS

Ruth 1:1–18   Hebrews 9:11–14
Psalm 146   Mark 12:28–34

OPENING SENTENCES

Sing praise to the Lord,
whose faithful love is forever,
who seeks justice for all of creation,
setting prisoners free,
lifting up those who are bowed down;
who watches over the estranged;
and who sustains those who are without care.

Sing praises to the one who loves the righteous
and frustrates the ways of the wicked.
Sing praise with all your life.

PRAYER OF THE DAY

Faithful God, even as we gather this day
we have many concerns that seek our attention.
Let us be present for you as you are present for us,
that in our attention we might catch a glimpse
of the perfect love you extend to us.
Let our hearts be made open
so that this love transforms us
for your purposes in the world. **Amen.**

But Ruth said, "Do not press me to leave you or to turn back from following you! Where you go, I will go; where you lodge, I will lodge; your people shall be my people, and your God my God."
Ruth 1:16

INVITATION TO DISCIPLESHIP

The invitation to discipleship may be led from the baptismal font.

Jesus has offered himself to each one of us
out of a faithful and abiding love
that is rooted in wholeness of life for all.

How will you respond?
Join him in this work,
and let it transform your soul
for the sake of a world
that hungers to be transformed by love.

PRAYERS OF INTERCESSION

The prayers of intercession may be led from the midst of the congregation.

Faithful God,
we confess to you that our faithfulness falls short
more often than we'd like.
We are grateful that you are a God of infinite chances.
As we try again,
we ask that you would meet us in our efforts—
not for our sakes,
but for the sake of the world you love.

For creation . . .
We marvel at the regenerative
and renewing work of your creation,
and we ask that you grant us the courage
to forfeit behaviors, systems, and structures
that introduce harm into your creation.
Help us to apply our minds and imaginations
to new ways of gleaning energy,
harvesting resources, and distributing goods.
Disrupt our habits of overconsumption,
and help us to be present
to the gifts you have given to us.

For our communities . . .
We grieve the ways in which
our social fabric has become frayed and ruptured.

Grant us self-awareness
to see the ways in which we participate in this relational harm
and to disrupt our practices of brokenness.
Grant us a spiritual generosity and commitment to you
as we seek to meet one another
with a faithful love that mirrors yours.

For this community . . .
For those among us
who are in the midst of depression or despair,
who are full of anxiety and fear,
grant us the courage to continue moving forward.
Lift our gaze to see who you are
and where you are inviting us to be.
Help us to help each other,
knowing that as we grab hold of one another's hands,
we are ourselves mutually transformed.

In your holy name we pray. **Amen.**

INVITATION TO OFFERING

The invitation to offering may be led from the Communion table.

All that we have comes from God.

As we offer our gifts today,
let them be signs of gratitude
and an act of faithfulness,
that what we give
might work to strengthen our spirits
and transform our communities.

INVITATION TO THE TABLE

The invitation to the table is led from the Communion table.

At this table we dine with those
who have hungered to know God's justice and faithfulness.
At this table we dine with those
who have worked toward God's justice and faithfulness.
At this table, whether we hunger or work,
we do so together—
bound by a faithful love that will not let us go.

CHARGE

The blessing and charge may be led from the doors of the church.

Go forward from this place,
remembering that God's faithful love
will never leave you.
Let that love transform, empower, and set you free
for a life that binds you
to those whom God has called you to love.
Amen. *or* **Thanks be to God.**

Proper 26

Sunday, October 30—November 5

COMPLEMENTARY READINGS

Deuteronomy 6:1–9   Hebrews 9:11–14
Psalm 119:1–8   Mark 12:28–34

OPENING SENTENCES

Hear, O people:
The Lord is our God,
the Lord alone.

We shall love the Lord
with all our heart, soul, and might.
We will keep these words in our hearts.
Let us worship God!

PRAYER OF THE DAY

O God,
we thank you for gathering us together.
Open our hearts and minds
to hear and understand your commandments.
Through your Holy Spirit
renew in us a desire to follow you
in heart, mind, and soul,
that we may love you and lift up your name.
In Christ we pray. **Amen.**

One of the scribes came near and heard them
disputing with one another, and seeing that
[Jesus] answered them well, he asked him,
"Which commandment is the first of all?"
Mark 12:28

INVITATION TO DISCIPLESHIP

The invitation to discipleship may be led from the baptismal font.

Jesus has called us
to love the Lord our God
with all our heart,
and with all our understanding,
and with all our strength,
and to love our neighbors as ourselves.

How will you live out your calling
in service to God and others?
If you are ready to live your full being
in this community of faith,
you are welcome here.

PRAYERS OF INTERCESSION

The prayers of intercession may be led from the midst of the congregation.

As we prepare to lift our prayers to God,
we know and trust that God hears us.
God of our salvation, **hear our prayer.**

For those who are suffering from illness . . .
God of our salvation, **hear our prayer.**

For all communities of faith that gather to worship you . . .
God of our salvation, **hear our prayer.**

For those who serve others with compassion and love . . .
God of our salvation, **hear our prayer.**

For those who are troubled and lonely . . .
God of our salvation, **hear our prayer.**

For those affected by war and conflict . . .
God of our salvation, **hear our prayer.**

We give you thanks, O Lord,
that you have heard our prayers.
Strengthen us to go forth and serve you
with confidence and joy.
In the name of Christ we pray. **Amen.**

INVITATION TO OFFERING

The invitation to offering may be led from the Communion table.

Let us offer our gifts with thanks and praise,
and put our trust in the Lord.

Through this offering
let us return to God a portion
of what God has graciously given to us.

INVITATION TO THE TABLE

The invitation to the table is led from the Communion table.

Beloved, we are invited to this table
to share the gifts of God
through this bread and cup.
We are not invited
because we believe ourselves to be worthy
or come from a certain race, religion, or nationality.
We are invited simply because
God took the initiative to love us first.

Come and partake of the feast
that Christ provides for us.

CHARGE

The blessing and charge may be led from the doors of the church.

Let us go forth to love God
and to love our neighbors as ourselves.
Amen. *or* **Thanks be to God.**

All Saints' Day

November 1 or the first Sunday in November

Wisdom 3:1–9 *or*   Revelation 21:1–6a
 Isaiah 25:6–9   John 11:32–44
Psalm 24

OPENING SENTENCES

Lift up your heads, O gates!
Be lifted up, you ancient doors!

Who is the one
who reigns in glory?
The Lord our God,
strong and mighty!

Lift up your heads, O gates!
Be lifted up, you ancient doors!

Who is the one
who reigns in glory?
The Lord our God,
now and always!

PRAYER OF THE DAY

Almighty God,
you alone have the power
to turn weeping into laughing,
to transform fear into faith,
to raise us from death to life.
Call us by our names,
release us from bondage,
and lead us forth into the light,
that we might sing your praise forever;
through Jesus Christ our Lord. **Amen.**

INVITATION TO DISCIPLESHIP

The invitation to discipleship may be led from the baptismal font.

Let me tell you a secret.
Saints are not spiritual superheroes.
Saints are just everyday disciples
who seek the grace of God every day.
Saints are just ordinary people
who share the extraordinary love of God.

Don't you want to be in that number?
Come and join us in this community of faith,
this company of everyday, ordinary people,
made holy by the Lord.

PRAYERS OF INTERCESSION

The prayers of intercession may be led from the midst of the congregation.

Holy One, Alpha and Omega,
hear our prayers.

For those who are waiting for deliverance
from captivity and oppression . . .
Show them your salvation.

For those who are living and serving
as members of Christ's body . . .
Raise them from the dead.

For those who are struggling and striving
for justice and reconciliation . . .
Deliver them from evil.

For those who are working and praying
for the healing of the earth . . .
Make all things new.

For those who are tormented and afflicted
by sickness, suffering, and sin . . .
Grant them your peace.

For those who are weeping and mourning
for loved ones they have lost . . .
Wipe away their tears.

Holy One, Alpha and Omega,
restore us from death to life,
and give us a place among the saints
who wait to welcome your new creation—
a new heaven and a new earth;
through Jesus Christ our Lord. **Amen.**

INVITATION TO OFFERING

The invitation to offering may be led from the Communion table.

With open hands and open hearts
we come before the Lord our God—
ready to join the work of Jesus,
ready to share the gifts of the Spirit,
ready to sing the song of the saints.

Let us offer our lives to the Lord.

INVITATION TO THE TABLE

The invitation to the table is led from the Communion table.

Rejoice, people of God!
The Lord wipes away our tears.
Give thanks, people of God!
The Lord takes away our shame.
Sing praise, people of God!
The Lord swallows up death forever.

This is the table of the Lord.
This is the day of salvation.
Come with the saints of all the ages.
Come and share this holy feast.

CHARGE

The blessing and charge may be led from the doors of the church.

Go and tell the good news of salvation.
Now the home of God is among us.
Even death has passed away.
God is making all things new.
Amen. *or* **Thanks be to God.**

Proper 27

Sunday, November 6–12

SEMICONTINUOUS READINGS

Ruth 3:1–5; 4:13–17   Hebrews 9:24–28
Psalm 127   Mark 12:38–44

OPENING SENTENCES

We gather here in a house
built not by our hands but by God.
**We gather here in a community
knit together not by creed or confession
but by Christ and Calvary.**

We gather here not to affirm our strength
but to confess our dependence
on the one in whom all things hang together.
**Let us worship God,
not by our own power
but in our need for a God
who can make all things right
and heal all wounds.**

PRAYER OF THE DAY

Loving God, meet us in this place.
Reveal your power,
even as we experience your passion.
Call us out of our self-obsession
to focus on your greater purpose,
that in this calling
we might know your great capacity
to do more within us and through us
than we could ever do on our own. **Amen.**

INVITATION TO DISCIPLESHIP

The invitation to discipleship may be led from the baptismal font.

Do you wish to find your future renewed?
Do you seek restoration in your deepest pain?

God invites you to step into the mystery of Christ
and be transformed by the power of love
for the sake of a world that needs to know more of it.

PRAYERS OF INTERCESSION

The prayers of intercession may be led from the midst of the congregation.

Eternal God,
Scripture tells us that your promises
carry from generation to generation
and your faithfulness is unending,
that you can work greatness
out of the humblest of circumstances
and awe amid the most grinding of days.
We need to know that this is true,
so we ask that you hear us today
as we lift up that which weighs heaviest on our hearts.

For those whose lives have been torn apart
by factors beyond their control,
for refugees fleeing the effects of war,
climate change, economic exploitation,
and all manner of government instability—
we pray your steadfast hand to make a way
where there seems to be no way,
that you would not only see the plight of those who suffer,
but move the hearts, minds, and monies
of those who are in a position to transform structures
and move resources for your purposes.

For those among us who struggle
with anxiety, loneliness, and vocational drift—
we ask that your Spirit guide us
as we journey through our wildernesses,
that even as we struggle to find our way forward
your calling voice would ring clearly enough
to draw us toward your purposes.
Help us in all things to trust your promises,
that we might be encouraged and empowered
to work toward their reality.

In your holy name we pray. **Amen.**

INVITATION TO OFFERING

The invitation to offering may be led from the Communion table.

At this time we have an opportunity
to offer what we have to God—
not out of abundance but out of faithfulness.

As you give of yourself,
let it be a sign of your faith that God provides,
not only for you but for this gathered community.

INVITATION TO THE TABLE

The invitation to the table is led from the Communion table.

We come to this table hewn by Christ's hands.
As both carpenter and custodian of the joyful feast,
he invites us to dine alongside one another
in friendship, faith, and thanksgiving.

Gather around this table,
remembering the goodness of God's provision
and the sustenance of God's grace.

CHARGE

The blessing and charge may be led from the doors of the church.

God sees the fullness of your story
and is not done writing it.
Go forth from this place in the knowledge
that there is a story yet to be written
through your faithfulness and flourishing,
in order that this world might flourish all the more.
Amen. *or* **Thanks be to God.**

Proper 27

Sunday, November 6–12

COMPLEMENTARY READINGS

1 Kings 17:8–16	Hebrews 9:24–28
Psalm 146	Mark 12:38–44

OPENING SENTENCES

Praise the Lord!
Praise the Lord, O my soul!

We will praise the Lord as long as we live.
**We will sing praises to God
for the rest of our lives.
Praise the Lord!**

PRAYER OF THE DAY

Faithful God, we thank you
for this day to gather together in worship.
You know us better than we know ourselves.
Cleanse us from all the things
that keep us from fully worshiping you.
By the power of the Holy Spirit,
embolden us to love and serve you.
We ask this in the name
of our Lord and Savior, Jesus Christ. **Amen.**

INVITATION TO DISCIPLESHIP

The invitation to discipleship may be led from the baptismal font.

Christ will come to save those
who are eagerly waiting for him.

If you have been waiting
to begin a relationship with Christ,
we invite you to become a part of this church.

PRAYERS OF INTERCESSION

The prayers of intercession may be led from the midst of the congregation.

According to the word of the Lord
spoken through the prophet Elijah,
"The jar of meal will not be emptied,
and the jug of oil will not fail."
As we lift up our joys and concerns to the Lord,
let us trust in God's sustaining work.
Let us pray.

For those suffering from hunger and thirst,
may they be filled . . .

For elected leaders,
may they govern according to your will . . .

For our churches,
may they be empowered by the Holy Spirit
to serve you in the world . . .

For those dealing with depression and mental illness,
may you bring healing . . .

For churches in Africa,
may they continue to bear witness to your works
and give you praise. . .

Loving God, receive our prayers.
Let us go forth in confidence,
trusting in your providence and mercy.
In the name of Jesus Christ we pray. **Amen.**

INVITATION TO OFFERING

The invitation to offering may be led from the Communion table.

Remember the words of Jesus
concerning a poor widow:
"For all of them have contributed
out of their abundance;
but she out of her poverty
has put in everything she had,
all she had to live on."

With all that we have and all that we are,
let us return our gifts to the Lord.

INVITATION TO THE TABLE

The invitation to the table is led from the Communion table.

You are welcome at this table.
Today, through the mercy and grace of God,
this meal of bread and wine is prepared for you.
People will come from all directions
and all walks of life
to gather as one body in Christ.

Come, eat at this table that is set for you.
Let us rejoice and be glad!

CHARGE

The blessing and charge may be led from the doors of the church.

The Lord will reign forever;
your God, O Zion, for all generations.
Amen. *or* **Thanks be to God.**

Proper 28

Sunday, November 13–19

SEMICONTINUOUS READINGS

1 Samuel 1:4–20   Hebrews 10:11–14 (15–18), 19–25
1 Samuel 2:1–10   Mark 13:1–8

OPENING SENTENCES

We come to this place
**bringing our deepest hopes
and our strongest fears.**

We come with rejoicing on our lips.
We come with sorrow in our hearts.

We come with trouble in our souls.
We come with gratitude in our eyes.

We come with all we are.
We come with faith and perseverance.

PRAYER OF THE DAY

Holy One,
help us to recognize you this day.
Help us to recognize you in our lives.
Help us to hold your word in us.
Help us to extend your grace to the world.
Help us to know you. **Amen.**

> *Hannah prayed and said, "My heart exults in the
> LORD; my strength is exalted in my God. My
> mouth derides my enemies, because I rejoice in
> your victory. There is no Holy One like the LORD,
> no one besides you; there is no Rock like our God."*
> *1 Samuel 2:1–2*

INVITATION TO DISCIPLESHIP

The invitation to discipleship may be led from the baptismal font.

The Holy Spirit says,
"This is the covenant I will make with them:
I will put my laws in their hearts.
I will write them on their minds.
I will remember their sins no more."

This fresh slate, this new direction,
is what God calls us to today.
Let us hold fast to our hope, without wavering.
Let us approach God with true hearts,
in full assurance of faith.
For God, who has promised, is faithful.

PRAYERS OF INTERCESSION

The prayers of intercession may be led from the midst of the congregation.

God who listens,
God who sees,
God who acts:

There is no wrong way to come to you.
We can come with dancing and praise,
and we can come with weeping and lament.
We can come feeling many things at once,
and we can come feeling nothing at all.

Today we are here.
We are here with our most exciting news,
with happiness that flows out of us.
We lift our joys to you now . . .

[Time is provided for people to name their joys.]

Today we are here.
We are here with our gut-wrenching disappointments,
with despair that threatens to swallow us.
We lift our concerns to you now . . .

[Time is provided for people to name their concerns.]

We come to your holy place
trusting that you listen,
trusting that you see,
trusting that you will act. **Amen.**

INVITATION TO OFFERING

The invitation to offering may be led from the Communion table.

God does see us—
when we are in distress,
when we feel secure and hopeful,
when we have little,
and when we have plenty.

No matter how we come here,
we offer what we can:
our resources, our time,
our skills, our prayers.

INVITATION TO THE TABLE

The invitation to the table is led from the Communion table.

We hear it again and again:
the first are made last,
the mighty break and the weak rise,
the rich are hungry and the poor are full.

This is the table where expectations are broken,
the supper where surprises are inevitable.
This is where our God meets us,
giving us seats of honor.
There is no one like God.
There is no mercy like God's.
There is no faithfulness like God's.

CHARGE

The blessing and charge may be led from the doors of the church.

Hold fast to God's love!
Amen. *or* **Thanks be to God.**

Proper 28

Sunday, November 13–19

COMPLEMENTARY READINGS

Daniel 12:1–3   Hebrews 10:11–14 (15–18), 19–25
Psalm 16   Mark 13:1–8

OPENING SENTENCES

The Lord is our chosen portion and cup.
Let us rejoice and worship God.

We bless the Lord, who gives us counsel.
Let us rejoice and worship God.

We keep the Lord always before us.
Therefore our hearts are glad.
Let us rejoice and worship God.

PRAYER OF THE DAY

Everlasting God,
we give you thanks for Jesus Christ,
your Son and our Savior.
Cleanse us through the Holy Spirit
from all things that prohibit
the hearing of your Word.
Renew in us hope and joy,
that we may serve you in this world.
We ask these things in the name of Jesus Christ. **Amen.**

> *You show me the path of life. In your presence
> there is fullness of joy; in your right hand are
> pleasures forevermore.*
> *Psalm 16:11*

INVITATION TO DISCIPLESHIP

The invitation to discipleship may be led from the baptismal font.

The psalmist says,
"You show me the path of life.
In your presence there is fullness of joy;
in your right hand are pleasures forevermore."

We serve a God who shows us the way to live.
If you have been led to respond
to God's calling in your life,
we will promise to walk with you on this journey.

PRAYERS OF INTERCESSION

The prayers of intercession may be led from the midst of the congregation.

Eternal God, hear us now
as we lift up our thanksgivings.

For food, shelter, and nurture . . .

For this church family . . .

For nature and all the creatures of the earth . . .

For family and friends . . .

For opportunities to serve . . .

God of glory, hear us now
as we lift up our concerns.

For those who are homeless and lost . . .

For those who are sick and homebound . . .

For our nation and leaders . . .

For those who have suffered from acts of violence. . .

God, hear our prayers.
Renew our confidence and trust in you,
that we may not be afraid or discouraged.
Prepare us for the joy of serving you
and your people in this world.
In the name of Christ we pray. **Amen.**

INVITATION TO OFFERING

The invitation to offering may be led from the Communion table.

A freewill offering is our sacrifice of praise.
Give thanks to God, whose name is good.

Let us offer our lives to the Lord.

INVITATION TO THE TABLE

The invitation to the table is led from the Communion table.

Friends, this is the joyful feast
of the people of God!
We serve a God who is gracious and merciful.
We are loved so much
that Jesus Christ has prepared this table for us.

Come and partake of these gifts,
for all God's people have a place at this table.
Blessed is the Lord our God!

CHARGE

The blessing and charge may be led from the doors of the church.

Let us hold fast to the confession of our hope
without wavering,
for the one who has promised is faithful.
Amen. *or* **Thanks be to God.**

Christ the King/Reign of Christ

Sunday, November 20–26

SEMICONTINUOUS READINGS

2 Samuel 23:1–7   Revelation 1:4b–8
Psalm 132:1–12 (13–18)   John 18:33–37

OPENING SENTENCES

Let us go to God's dwelling place;
let us worship at God's footstool.

Rise up, O Lord, and go to your resting place,
you and the ark of your might.

Let your priests be clothed with righteousness,
and let your faithful shout for joy.

PRAYER OF THE DAY

We praise you, our God and Sovereign,
and bless your name forever and ever.
Previous generations have told us of your works,
and we shall declare your mighty acts
to those who come after us.
All creation praises you, O Lord,
and all your faithful people bless you and give thanks.
We shall speak of the glory of your realm
and tell of your power. **Amen.**

The God of Israel has spoken, the Rock of Israel has said to me: One who rules over people justly, ruling in the fear of God, is like the light of morning, like the sun rising on a cloudless morning, gleaming from the rain on the grassy land.
2 Samuel 23:3–4

INVITATION TO DISCIPLESHIP

The invitation to discipleship may be led from the baptismal font.

When questioned about his kingdom,
Jesus answered, "You say that I am a king.
For this I was born,
and for this I came into the world,
to testify to the truth.
Everyone who belongs to the truth
listens to my voice."

The voice of Jesus, our shepherd,
is speaking today, calling us into truth.
How will you respond to that call?

PRAYERS OF INTERCESSION

The prayers of intercession may be led from the midst of the congregation.

Holy One,
you came down to earth with divine joy*
and lived among us, full of grace and truth.
Live in our hearts,
that we may be your humble dwelling
and agents of your peace in your holy realm.

Jesus, you are all compassion
and are filled with pure, unbounded love.
Into every trembling heart
bring your peace.
Into every troubled heart
breathe your loving Spirit,
that we may find rest for our souls.

Earthly rulers fail us,
and our kingdoms
are but a shadow of your realm.
May we not equate our political successes
with your sovereign love.
Give us humble hearts,
that we may worship you
and not ourselves. **Amen.**

* This prayer is inspired by the Charles Wesley hymn "Love Divine, All Loves Excelling."

INVITATION TO OFFERING

The invitation to offering may be led from the Communion table.

God's reign is unlike that of earthly kings.
In God's economy there is enough for all
and justice for everyone.
Through our work and our witness
we seek to testify to the abundant mercy of God,
giving people a glimpse
of a different way of living together
in a peaceable kingdom.

As our offering is received this morning,
let us give of our time, treasure, and talent
in hope that we can all experience God's abundant love.

INVITATION TO THE TABLE

The invitation to the table is led from the Communion table.

King David really wanted to build a home for God.
"I will not enter my house," he said,
"or get into my bed;
I will not give sleep to my eyes
or slumber to my eyelids,
until I find a place for the Lord,
a dwelling place for the Mighty One of Jacob."
The temple would be his son Solomon's project,
and it was glorious, but it would come to an end,
in the way of all human-built projects.
David wanted to give God a home among mortals.
God accomplished that,
not with walls of solid stone
but in the fragile, human life of Jesus.

At this table we glimpse God's reign—
where permanence and strength
don't come from human might and engineering
but from the power of God's love,
transcending death itself.
At this table we glimpse God's abundance—
where nobody is turned away,
because there is always room for another seat.
At this table we glimpse God's mercy.
We are invited here
not because we are more worthy than others
but because God's desire is to feed the world.
So come and be fed.
There is room for you here.

CHARGE

The blessing and charge may be led from the doors of the church.

Jesus said his kingdom was not of this world.
But this is the world in which we live
and to which we are called.
So go into the world
and live as if God's kingdom has already been realized.
Remember that there is enough for all
if we're willing to share it.
Remember that there are no conditions on God's love for you,
and offer that same love to others.
Remember that justice is at the heart of God,
and work to make it visible
in the hearts of those you encounter.
Go in love to serve
and to show God's peaceable kingdom.
Amen. *or* **Thanks be to God.**

Christ the King/Reign of Christ

Sunday, November 20–26

COMPLEMENTARY READINGS

Daniel 7:9–10, 13–14   Revelation 1:4b–8
Psalm 93   John 18:33–37

OPENING SENTENCES

Grace be to you . . .
Look! God is coming with the clouds!

. . . and peace from the one . . .
Every eye will see! Every ear will hear!

. . . who was, and is, and is to come.
God is the Alpha and Omega! Alleluia!

PRAYER OF THE DAY

We have come to your house, O God,
to your resting place,
because here we feel near to you.
You are everywhere,
reigning over all things,
close to us in your sanctuary
and far enough away
to watch the planets move.
Help us to feel your presence
renewing and reenergizing us,
here in this place and in all the world. **Amen.**

Grace to you and peace from him who is and who was and
who is to come, and from the seven spirits who are before
his throne, and from Jesus Christ, the faithful witness, the
firstborn of the dead, and the ruler of the kings of the earth.
Revelation 1:4b–5a

INVITATION TO DISCIPLESHIP

The invitation to discipleship may be led from the baptismal font.

We enter any space of worship
carrying our preconceived ideas of who God is—
the image of God our parents painted for us,
the ideas we picked up from church and culture,
the experiences we carry, filled with joy and pain.
But Jesus makes it clear.
Beyond what the world says, Jesus says,
"For this I was born,
and for this I came into the world:
to testify to the truth."

What is the truth you are hearing in your heart?
What keeps you from listening to Christ's voice?
What needs to shift to deepen your discipleship?

PRAYERS OF INTERCESSION

The prayers of intercession may be led from the midst of the congregation.

Almighty and Everlasting God,
your kin-dom may not be of this world,
but we are living in this world—
a world where rulers are not always just,
a world where oppression takes hold.

We know that you are above all things
yet an intimate part of our lives.
We know this, but it is hard to live in the truth.
It is hard to believe that the day will ever come
when your will is done on earth
as it is in heaven.

But that is what we pray for.
That is what we are called to strive for.
That is what you tell us the world could be.

Guide us as we work for that world.
Help us to keep walking by faith.
Restore us when we lose heart or health.
Help us to share when we have more than enough.

Hold us to the prayers we pray
and to the words we profess to believe,
that the day may soon come
when all shall see, feel, and know
the beautiful kin-dom of God. **Amen.**

INVITATION TO OFFERING

The invitation to offering may be led from the Communion table.

God has made with us an everlasting covenant,
showering us with loving-kindness,
leading us toward truth.

Here in God's house
we offer these gifts of gratitude back to God.

INVITATION TO THE TABLE

The invitation to the table is led from the Communion table.

Jesus Christ—
the beginning and the end,
the Almighty,
the faithful witness,
the firstborn of the dead,
the ruler of the rulers of the earth;

Jesus Christ—
who was and is,
who is to come,
who loves us,
who freed us from sin,
who made us to be a beloved community;

this Jesus Christ
has set this table for us,
has drawn up invitations for us,
has come to join us—
in fellowship,
in forgiveness,
in feasting.

CHARGE

The blessing and charge may be led from the doors of the church.

Go forth, belonging to the truth!
Let us listen for God's voice!
Amen. *or* **Thanks be to God.**

Supplements for the
Narrative Lectionary

1 Kings 12:1–17, 25–29

Narrative Lectionary Year 2, 8
(with Mark 10:42–45)

OPENING SENTENCES

Those who love me
I will deliver, says the Lord.
**I will protect those
who know my name.**

When they call to me
I will answer them.
I will be with them in trouble.

I will rescue them and honor them.
**With long life I will satisfy them
and show them my salvation.**

PRAYER OF THE DAY

Holy One,
you have led your people
from captivity to freedom,
that we might serve you alone.
Put down tyrants,
liberate the oppressed,
and govern us with grace,
that all may have life and joy;
through Jesus Christ our Lord. **Amen.**

INVITATION TO DISCIPLESHIP

The invitation to discipleship may be led from the baptismal font.

We are called to be humble servants,
following the example of our servant Lord.
As Jesus teaches us,
"Whoever wishes to be great among you
must be your servant."

We invite you to join us in this calling—
to offer your life in love and service
to our God and to our neighbors.

PRAYERS OF INTERCESSION

The prayers of intercession may be led from the midst of the congregation.

Holy God,
you are sovereign and savior of the nations.
Receive our prayers for the peoples of the earth.

For lands where tyrants reign . . .
Break the grip of violence and terror;
cast down the mighty from their thrones.
Hear our prayer: **Deliver us from evil.**

For victims of abuse and torture . . .
Protect those who are most vulnerable;
give them safety and heal their wounds.
Hear our prayer: **Deliver us from evil.**

For those subjected to cruel insults . . .
Silence the lips that spew hatred;
teach us to bless and not to curse.
Hear our prayer: **Deliver us from evil.**

For those captivated by false idols . . .
Help us to turn away from temptation;
call us to worship you alone.
Hear our prayer: **Deliver us from evil.**

For nations and peoples divided . . .
Dismantle the walls of hostility;
show us the path to reconciliation.
Hear our prayer: **Deliver us from evil.**

Holy God,
your way is righteous,
your realm is just,
and your promise is peace.
Lead us to your kingdom,
where there is abundant life for all;
through Jesus Christ our Lord. **Amen.**

INVITATION TO OFFERING

The invitation to offering may be led from the Communion table.

Christ has called us to use our gifts
in the service of others.

With great thanksgiving for God's grace
let us offer our lives to the Lord.

INVITATION TO THE TABLE

The invitation to the table is led from the Communion table.

Christ calls us to this table,
and here he serves us—
feeding us with his own body and blood.
We go forth from this meal
to serve our neighbors—
sharing our lives in acts of love and care.

Come to the table
to be nourished and served.
Then go to the world
to feed and serve others in Jesus' name.

CHARGE

The blessing and charge may be led from the doors of the church.

Remember the words of Jesus:
"Whoever wishes to be first among you
must be the servant of all."
Let us love and serve the Lord.
Amen. *or* **Thanks be to God.**

2 Kings 22:1–10 (11–20); 23:1–3

Narrative Lectionary Year 2, 12
(with Luke 24:30–32)

OPENING SENTENCES

Let us turn to the Lord our God
with all our heart and soul.
Let us keep God's commandments
and study the book of the law.

Is the word of God too difficult for us,
too far away or beyond our reach?
No, the word of God is near to us,
on our lips and in our hearts.

God has given us a choice this day:
life or death, blessings or curses.
Let us choose life, that we may live.
Let us follow the word of the Lord.

PRAYER OF THE DAY

Holy One,
you have provided your people
with the book of Scripture
to be our way of truth and life.
Teach us by your Word
and lead us through your Spirit,
that we may follow you faithfully;
through Jesus Christ our Lord. **Amen.**

The invitation to discipleship may be led from the baptismal font.

> In every generation we are called
> to return to the word of the Lord—
> to claim in our own lives
> the promises and challenges of faith.
>
> How will you receive God's Word?
> How will you respond to God's call?

PRAYERS OF INTERCESSION

The prayers of intercession may be led from the midst of the congregation.

> God of all wisdom,
> we give you thanks
> that you still speak to us through Scripture
> and listen to us through prayer.
> Receive our prayers for your church and world.
>
> For the leaders and people of the church . . .
> Open our minds to understand your teaching;
> stir our hearts to share your love.
> Hear our prayer: **Let your will be done.**
>
> For the leaders and people of all nations . . .
> Teach them the paths of righteousness;
> show them the ways of justice and peace.
> Hear our prayer: **Let your will be done.**
>
> For places affected by disaster . . .
> Rescue those who are in danger;
> restore broken communities to wholeness.
> Hear our prayer: **Let your will be done.**
>
> For those who are in need . . .
> Provide abundantly for people who are poor;
> make us generous to share what we have.
> Hear our prayer: **Let your will be done.**

For all who are sick and suffering . . .
Heal and comfort those who are hurting;
strengthen those who care for others.
Hear our prayer: **Let your will be done.**

God of all wisdom,
continue to speak to us.
Help us, day by day,
to seek and serve your purpose,
until your will is done
on earth as it is in heaven;
through Jesus Christ our Lord. **Amen.**

INVITATION TO OFFERING

The invitation to offering may be led from the Communion table.

The Lord has opened for us
all the treasures of heavenly wisdom
through the words of Scripture.

Let us open our hearts and hands
to love and serve the Lord.

INVITATION TO THE TABLE

The invitation to the table is led from the Communion table.

On the road to Emmaus, Jesus took bread,
blessed and broke it, and gave it to his disciples.
Then their eyes were opened
and they recognized him.
They said to each other,
"Were not our hearts burning within us
while he was talking to us on the road,
while he was opening the scriptures to us?"

Come to the table of the Lord.
Come and be nourished by Christ,
the Word of God made flesh.

The blessing and charge may be led from the doors of the church.

Keep listening for the word of the Lord,
and proclaim the good news to all the world.
Amen. *or* **Thanks be to God.**

Ezra 1:1–4; 3:1–4, 10–13

Narrative Lectionary Year 2, 15
(with Luke 2:25–32)

OPENING SENTENCES

Give thanks to the Lord, for God is good;
God's steadfast love endures forever!

Open to us the gates of righteousness;
let us go in and praise the Lord.

The stone that the builders rejected
has become the chief cornerstone.
This is the Lord's doing;
it is marvelous in our eyes.

This is the day that the Lord has made;
let us rejoice and be glad in it.

Give thanks to the Lord, for God is good;
God's steadfast love endures forever!

PRAYER OF THE DAY

Holy One,
you have gathered us in
from the disgrace of exile
and have given us a new home
in the glory of your presence.
Build up your church
as a place of sanctuary and service,
that all the world may come
to give you thanks and praise;
through Jesus Christ our Lord. **Amen.**

INVITATION TO DISCIPLESHIP

The invitation to discipleship may be led from the baptismal font.

This community of faith is called to be
the household of God,
the body of Christ,
and a temple of the Holy Spirit.
God is building us up.
Christ is knitting us together.
The Spirit is filling us with life.

We invite you to join this community,
to take part in what God is doing.
There is a place for you here.

PRAYERS OF INTERCESSION

The prayers of intercession may be led from the midst of the congregation.

God of glory,
you called us and claimed us as your people
even before you set the foundation of the earth.
Receive our prayers for the world you love.

For your church in every place . . .
Build us up as Christ's body;
equip us for ministry with Jesus.
Hear our prayer: **Hallowed be your name.**

For our neighbors of other faiths, or no faith . . .
Bless them with goodness and prosperity;
keep them in safety and peace.
Hear our prayer: **Hallowed be your name.**

For those who are living in exile . . .
Lead them to places of welcome;
help all people to find a home in you.
Hear our prayer: **Hallowed be your name.**

For the leaders of the nations . . .
Let them use their power for good;
guide them to serve your purpose.
Hear our prayer: **Hallowed be your name.**

For the earth that is our home . . .
Restore the health of this planet;
renew the life of the world.
Hear our prayer: **Hallowed be your name.**

God of glory,
open wide the doors of your house,
gather up the peoples of the earth,
and fit us for our heavenly home,
that we may glimpse your new creation;
through Jesus Christ our Lord. **Amen.**

INVITATION TO OFFERING

The invitation to offering may be led from the Communion table.

All the gifts of the people of God are needed
for building up this community of faith
and for the work of Christ's mission in the world.

Let us present to God the offering of our life and labor.

INVITATION TO THE TABLE

The invitation to the table is led from the Communion table.

This is a festival day!
Jesus Christ is the cornerstone of the church,
and Christ is risen from the dead.

Come, people of God.
Let us share the joyful feast
that Christ has prepared for us.

CHARGE

The blessing and charge may be led from the doors of the church.

Let us go now in peace,
according to God's word,
for our eyes have seen God's saving work,
prepared in the presence of all peoples:
light to the nations
and glory for the people of God.
Amen. *or* **Thanks be to God.**

Esther 4:1–17

Narrative Lectionary Year 1, 14
(with Matthew 5:13–16)

OPENING SENTENCES

Our help is in the name of the Lord,
maker of heaven and earth.

If the Lord had not been on our side,
our enemies would have swallowed us alive
and the flood would have swept us away.

Blessed be the Lord;
God will not give us up to death.

Our help is in the name of the Lord,
maker of heaven and earth.

PRAYER OF THE DAY

Holy One,
throughout the ages
you have saved us from destruction.
Help us to discern our calling
for just such a time as this,
that we may speak up for what is right,
defend those who are in trouble,
and prepare the way for your just reign;
through Jesus Christ our Lord. **Amen.**

INVITATION TO DISCIPLESHIP

The invitation to discipleship may be led from the baptismal font.

Jesus said, "You are the salt of the earth."
"You are the light of the world."
How will you add flavor and life to the world?
How will you let your light shine before others?

We invite you to join this community of faith
as we seek to follow Jesus together.

PRAYERS OF INTERCESSION

The prayers of intercession may be led from the midst of the congregation.

God our deliverer,
you answer the cries of your people
and defend the cause of the poor.
Receive our prayers for a world in crisis.

For all who are persecuted . . .
Put an end to acts of violence;
provide safe places for those in trouble.
Hear our prayer: **Save us from the time of trial.**

For all who are despised . . .
Dismantle systems of discrimination;
untangle patterns of prejudice.
Hear our prayer: **Save us from the time of trial.**

For all who are exploited . . .
Liberate those long held captive;
grant justice for those who are oppressed.
Hear our prayer: **Save us from the time of trial.**

For all who are vulnerable . . .
Shelter those who are unhoused;
protect those who are abused.
Hear our prayer: **Save us from the time of trial.**

For all who are afraid . . .
Give courage to the faint of heart;
give power to the weak.
Hear our prayer: **Save us from the time of trial.**

God our deliverer,
turn our prayers into action
for the sake of those in need.
Reveal to us your purpose
for just such a time as this;
through Jesus Christ our Lord. **Amen.**

INVITATION TO OFFERING

The invitation to offering may be led from the Communion table.

God has summoned us
to this time and this place
to help someone,
to change something,
to make a difference in the world.

Trusting in God's good purpose,
let us offer our lives to the Lord.

INVITATION TO THE TABLE

The invitation to the table is led from the Communion table.

The time for fasting and weeping has passed.
The time for feasting and rejoicing has come.
At this table we celebrate Christ's victory
over the powers of evil and death.
At this table we give thanks to God
for the gift of our salvation.

Come and share this joyful feast.

CHARGE

The blessing and charge may be led from the doors of the church.

Let your light shine before others,
that all may see your good works
and give glory to God.
Amen. *or* **Thanks be to God.**

Scripture Index

This is an index to the lectionary readings supported in this volume. Revised Common Lectionary readings are listed in regular type; supplemental readings for the Narrative Lectionary are listed in italics.

Comprehensive Scripture Index for Year B

This is an index to the lectionary readings supported in volumes 1 and 2 for Year B. Revised Common Lectionary readings are listed in regular type; supplemental readings for the Narrative Lectionary are listed in italics.

OLD TESTAMENT

Genesis

1:1–5	73 (B1)
1:1–2:4a	154 (B1)
2:18–24	169 (B2)
3:8–15	48 (B2)
7:1–5, 11–18; 8:6–18; 9:8–13	154 (B1)
9:8–17	126 (B1)
17:1–7, 15–16	129 (B1)
22:1–18	154 (B1)

Exodus

12:1–4 (5–10), 11–14	147 (B1)
14:10–31; 15:20–21	154 (B1)
15:1b–13, 17–18	154 (B1)
16:2–4, 9–15	106 (B2)
20:1–17	132 (B1)

Numbers

11:4–6, 10–16, 24–29	162 (B2)
21:4–9	135 (B1)

Deuteronomy

4:1–2, 6–9	132 (B2)
5:12–15	103 (B1), 41 (B2)
6:1–9	195 (B2)
18:15–20	84 (B1)
32:1–4, 7, 36a, 43a	154 (B1)

Joshua

24:1–2a, 14–18	126 (B2)

Ruth

1:1–18	191 (B2)
3:1–5; 4:13–17	202 (B2)

1 Samuel

1:4–20	209 (B2)
2:1–10	209 (B2)
3:1–10 (11–20)	77 (B1), 37 (B2)
8:4–11 (12–15), 16–20 (11:14–15)	44 (B2)
15:34–16:13	51 (B2)
17:(1a, 4–11, 19–23) 32–49	58 (B2)
17:57–18:5, 10–16	58 (B2)

2 Samuel

1:1, 17–27	66 (B2)
5:1–5, 9–10	74 (B2)
6:1–5, 12b–19	81 (B2)
7:1–11, 16	28 (B1)
7:1–14a	88 (B2)
11:1–15	95 (B2)
11:26–12:13a	102 (B2)
18:5–9, 15, 31–33	109 (B2)
23:1–7	215 (B2)

1 Kings

2:10–12; 3:3–14	116 (B2)
8:(1, 6, 10–11) 22–30,	
41–43	123 (B2)
12:1–17, 25–29	*225 (B2)*
17:8–16	206 (B2)
19:4–8	113 (B2)

2 Kings

2:1–12	108 (B1)
4:42–44	99 (B2)
5:1–14	92 (B1)
22:1–10 (11–20); 23:1–3	*228 (B2)*

Ezra

1:1–4; 3:1–4, 10–13	*232 (B2)*

Esther

4:1–17	*235 (B2)*
7:1–6, 9–10; 9:20–22	158 (B2)

Job

1:1; 2:1–10	165 (B2)
23:1–9, 16–17	172 (B2)
38:1–11	62 (B2)
38:1–7 (34–41)	179 (B2)
42:1–6, 10–17	185 (B2)

Psalms

1	196 (B1), 149 (B2)
4	179 (B1)
8	169 (B2)
9:9–20	58 (B2)
14	95 (B2)
15	132 (B2)
16	154 (B1), 212 (B2)
19	132, 154 (B1), 142 (B2)
19:7–14	162 (B2)
20	51 (B2)
22	150 (B1)
22:1–15	172 (B2)
22:23–31	129 (B1)
22:25–31	185 (B1)
23	182 (B1), 92 (B2)
24	81, 198 (B2)
25:1–10	126 (B1)

26	165 (B2)
29	73 (B1), 29 (B2)
30	92 (B1), 70 (B2)
31:9–16	142 (B1)
34:1–8	113 (B2)
34:1–8 (19–22)	185 (B2)
34:9–14	120 (B2)
34:15–22	126 (B2)
36:7–9	*214 (B1)*
41	95 (B1)
42	154 (B1)
43	154 (B1)
45:1–2, 6–9	129 (B2)
46	154 (B1)
47	192 (B1)
48	74 (B2)
50:1–6	108 (B1)
51:1–12	138 (B1), 102 (B2)
51:1–17	122 (B1)
54	154 (B2)
62:5–12	81 (B1)
72:1–7, 10–14	61 (B1)
78:23–29	106 (B2)
80:1–7, 17–19	17 (B1)
81:1–10	103 (B1), 41 (B2)
84	123 (B2)
85:1–2, 8–13	21 (B1)
85:8–13	85 (B2)
86:8–13	*211 (B1)*
89:1–4	*205 (B1)*
89:1–4, 19–26	28 (B1)
89:20–37	88 (B2)
90:12–17	175 (B2)
91:9–16	182 (B2)
92:1–4, 12–15	54 (B2)
93	192 (B1), 219 (B2)
96	39 (B1)
97	43 (B1)
98	47, 154, 188 (B1)
103:1–13, 22	99 (B1), 33 (B2)
104:1–9, 24, 35c	179 (B2)
104:24–34, 35b	199 (B1)
107:1–3, 17–22	135 (B1)
107:1–3, 23–32	62 (B2)
111	84 (B1), 116 (B2)
114	154, 172 (B1)
116:1–2, 12–19	147 (B1)

Psalms (*continued*)

116:1–9	145 (B2)
118:1–2, 14–24	168 (B1)
118:1–2, 19–29	142 (B1)
119:1–8	195 (B2)
119:9–16	138 (B1)
123	78 (B2)
124	158 (B2)
125	135 (B2)
126	25 (B1), 188 (B2)
127	202 (B2)
130	48, 66, 109 (B2)
131	*208 (B1)*
132:1–12 (13–18)	215 (B2)
133	176 (B1), 58 (B2)
136:1–9, 23–26	154 (B1)
138	44 (B2)
139:1–6, 13–18	77 (B1), 37 (B2)
143	154 (B1)
145:10–18	99 (B2)
146	139, 191, 206 (B2)
147:1–11, 20c	88 (B1)
147:12–20	56 (B1)
148	51 (B1)

Proverbs

1:20–33	142 (B2)
8:1–8, 19–21; 9:4b–6	154 (B1)
9:1–6	120 (B2)
22:1–2, 8–9, 22–23	135 (B2)
31:10–31	149 (B2)

Song of Solomon

2:8–13	129 (B2)

Isaiah

6:1–8	29 (B2)
9:2–7	39 (B1)
12:2–6	154 (B1)
25:6–9	168, 172 (B1), 198 (B2)
35:4–7a	139 (B2)
40:1–11	21 (B1)
40:21–31	88 (B1)
43:18–25	95 (B1)
50:4–9a	142 (B1), 145 (B2)
52:7–10	47 (B1)
52:13–53:12	150 (B1)

53:4–12	182 (B2)
55:1–11	154 (B1)
58:1–12	122 (B1)
60:1–6	61 (B1)
61:1–4, 8–11	25 (B1)
61:1–4, 9–11	154 (B1)
61:10–62:3	51 (B1)
62:6–12	43 (B1)
64:1–9	17 (B1)

Jeremiah

11:18–20	154 (B2)
23:1–6	92 (B2)
31:7–9	188 (B2)
31:7–14	56 (B1)
31:31–34	138 (B1)

Lamentations

3:22–33	70 (B2)

Ezekiel

2:1–5	78 (B2)
17:22–24	54 (B2)
36:24–28	154 (B1)
37:1–14	154, 199 (B1)

Daniel

3:1–29	154 (B1)
7:9–10, 13–14	219 (B2)
12:1–3	212 (B2)

Hosea

2:14–20	99 (B1), 33 (B2)

Joel

2:1–2, 12–17	122 (B1)

Amos

5:6–7, 10–15	175 (B2)
7:7–15	85 (B2)

Jonah

1:1–2:1	154 (B1)
2:2–3 (4–6), 7–9	154 (B1)
3:1–5, 10	81 (B1)

Zephaniah

3:14–20	154 (B1)

Contributors

CLAUDIA L. AGUILAR RUBALCAVA, Director of Engagement, More Light Presbyterians

MAMIE BROADHURST, Co-Pastor, University Presbyterian Church, Baton Rouge, Louisiana

DAVID GAMBRELL, Associate for Worship, Office of Theology and Worship, Presbyterian Mission Agency, Presbyterian Church (U.S.A.), Louisville, Kentucky

MARCI AULD GLASS, Pastor and Head of Staff, Calvary Presbyterian Church, San Francisco

MARCUS A. HONG, Director of Field Education and Assistant Professor of Practical Theology, Louisville Presbyterian Theological Seminary, Louisville, Kentucky

KIMBERLY BRACKEN LONG, Liturgical Scholar, Cambridge, Maryland

EMILY MCGINLEY, Senior Pastor, City Church, San Francisco

KENDRA L. BUCKWALTER SMITH, Director of the Worship Program, Pittsburgh Theological Seminary, and Associate Pastor for Discipleship, Shadyside Presbyterian Church, Pittsburgh, Pennsylvania

SAMUEL SON, Manager of Diversity and Reconciliation, Executive Director's Office, Presbyterian Mission Agency, Presbyterian Church (U.S.A.), Louisville, Kentucky

SLATS TOOLE, Freelance Writer, Minneapolis

BYRON A. WADE, General Presbyter, Presbytery of Western North Carolina, Morganton, North Carolina

Printed in the USA
CPSIA information can be obtained
at www.ICGtesting.com
CBHW021231110224
4073CB00002BA/1

9 780664 264956